# *If*
# THIS HOUSE
# Could Talk...

H L   D a h m e r

◆ FriesenPress

Suite 300 - 990 Fort St
Victoria, BC, V8V 3K2
Canada

www.friesenpress.com

ISBN
978-1-5255-8290-5 (Hardcover)
978-1-5255-8289-9 (Paperback)
978-1-5255-8291-2 (eBook)

*1. Biography & Autobiography, Personal Memoirs*

Distributed to the trade by The Ingram Book Company

Allow me to introduce myself. A middle-aged, retired, trying to keep it together mom, ex wife, widow, kinda-sorta Grandma and sometime achiever. Some lifetimes are easier than others. Since the passing of my husband, I try to spend most of the winter months down south and the rest of the partly cloudy season at my home by the lake. Blackflies and squirrels notwithstanding, it is a beautiful place to be.

This season, unlike every other before, I returned home in a world of lockdown, concern and fear of the unknown. An uneasy, surreal drive north with not much to offer in the way of food and humanity, crossing the border was a release of emotional tension. Also, unlike so many others arriving, I returned home to a nearly empty house. I mean it. No furniture except "my old piano", as Burton Cummings would say, a Saran-wrapped tv cabinet, an empty dining room buffet and a couple of beds with no sheets.

I felt displaced with the sudden rush to return home nearly a month early and with the current conditions of social distance in place, no way to rectify my personal empty nest. My own children grown and gone, my personal life finding a way to mess me up frequently, an empty house was not, as they say, done in the best circles.

I decided I would share a few smiles about my situation with my fellow online amigos and it has become my morning coffee solace. Welcome to Chuckles for the Caffeine Challenged.

My nearly empty house? In my most recent prior life, meaning the previous two years, I had thought to pursue nuptuals once more, only to find at the time, it wasn't working out. Friends who needed a temporary home were staying in my house, while I was spending the majority of my time feeling like WKRP In Cincinnatti. The packing and unpacking was taking its toll and with all of us seemingly moving at the same time, it was time to store my stuff and go south.

Moving forward into now, arriving home to an empty home, can have its advantages. You don't like this or that? No problem, just don't bring it back in. Want to change a few things? Great, do it while the place is empty. That is all fine and dandy until you need something that isn't there or you return to a world where you are unable to get your things from storage without involving others and to where you cannot get help in to shove around the things you do have.

Camping in Place

When I say the house was empty, I mean it.

So as I'm wondering and wandering today, I figured I'd try to find the sheets so I can make a cozy bed for tonight. Last two nights have been on the couch in front of the heater. The two propane heat stoves had refused to start for my good neighbours, helping me out prior to my arrival, so I had to be coached by the technician on "Starting Your Stove" 101 over the phone. Got it, through perseverance and dumb luck. Since the heat is now working, I thought a bed might be in order. In the bedroom, is my naked bed. Too cold to be naked myself, I anxiously search high and low for the fleece sheets. I find some, but they are large twin sized, made to fit the king size bed in the front porch. Way too cold for summer front porch sleeping. Kind of like a Florida room but this ain't Florida.

I look at the sheets trying to figure out how I can make them stretch to fit my vintage 1928 ¾ bed which is a double bed, due to the lovely, fairly new mattress on it that hangs so invitingly over the rails. Comfy though it may be, warm and fuzzy it's not. I think it's a no go. I could maybe use the two flat sheets and stretch them over the mattress, kind of like a cozy ground sheet when you are winter camping. Hey, thinks I, then I could put my sleeping bag over top and be warm as toast. I'm not sure why they say "warm as toast". Toast is only warm til it hits the plate. It should be "warm as long as you leave it in the toaster". But, I digress. I continue sheet searching on an epic scale. Box in the shed: no. Drawer in the buffet: no. Under the bed, the teeny tiny closet…nope nada nuttin. So, I muse to myself (in self isolation I'm the only one I can turn to for answers. You can already see how well that's working) but where else could they be??

Finally, it dawns on me that those sheets, along with the aforementioned sleeping bag (I kid you not) are in Florida…..

I had them with me and took them down, forgetting a) that they were in the car and b) that here is where I'd need both of the damn things - not down there.

Couch Zone - Night 3
Stay Tuned for more As the House Spins…or Heather Gets it Together…..

# CHAPTER 2
## FINDING YOUR CUTLERY…

When you move out and take all your stuff with you, one would think that when you come back, so does your stuff. Oh no, friends, not during a 14 day self-quarantine, it doesn't. You never think that when you return, you can't get your stuff. When I arrived here Friday around 4, I had enough food and necessities from the trip to get by. No cooking required at that time. More groceries delivered Saturday morning. By yesterday, done with trying to get organized, I started to look for stuff. Nothing here, nothing there…nothing up my sleeve..presto! No utensils…no stuff.

Then, I began to search in earnest. Ernest didn't have it, either. Remembering that lots of stuff is in storage in various places, I start digging in the shed. Looking for anything I can use to fry, bake or mix with. I find an antique hand mixer, no cord so that tells you how old it is. Next, a pair of salt & peppers. That's not useful at all…there are another 860 pairs with nothing in them either. Sigh. Then I hit the mother lode…a box of cutlery, complete with ice cream scoop and a toaster. Wait til I get that sucker inside. Toast!!! I can have toast! I want to know which side toasts faster and how long each flap needs to be up before the toast burns. Who wouldn't?? So I lug it in the house, carefully crossing no one's path from the shed to the door (10 yards) in my empty yard. Since I've been socially distanced from everything I own for about 6 months already, I think I've got this.

Eager and excited to see what's in the rest of the four boxes, I start opening them up. Paper flying, tape ripping and there's dishes, bowls, fry pan and more lids. The pans that go with them are nowhere to be found but hey, I've got lids, it's a start!

Washing, soaking then put away…I think I'll save more Isolation Games for another day.

# CHAPTER 3

## A TALE OF TWO SHOES....

Today's tale is yet another shed scavenging soirée deep into the abyss of the no-person land behind my house. Get your coffee, come a little closer to the screen (but not too close, you know the rules) and open your ears while I share a sordid saga of dread and despair.....listen up, my lovelies for this is a sad, old story, one of loss and longing, the unrequited love of two soles stuck in everlasting, unending separation.

It all began, one warm and sunny November day in the Beforetime. You remember those days....Golfing, hugging, beaching, sitting and visiting, drinking...we can still do the drinking part just not all together as we did. So, I find a black shoe in my closet. I had half wondered, throughout my unpacking and unloading, where in the effn lord the other shoe was. I have this lovely pair of black Nike golf shoes (I know they're Nike...they're all swooped and everything) and for some reason, I can only find one shoe. I don't give it too much more thought at the time, being eager to get on with golfing, beaching and so forth and eventually forget about it. I come across it now and then, over the season and think, oh my, I simply must find that other shoe but, I don't. I carry on, doing all the things then, suddenly, I have to go home. Now, I start quickly packing and so forth and guess what? I come across this one shoe. Again. Same shoe, different day. Half a pair, as it were. It were only an 'alf as it ain't an whole. I stare at the shoe, that little smirking piece of leather, thinking, to myself of course, because you know if you talk to yourself, everybody will think you're nuts. Why open your mouth and remove all doubt? So I'm busy thinking, once again, "Where can that other &$@# shoe be?" So in the end, I leave it there as I'm really cramped for room and don't want to haul one shoe 1,872km or 1,163.2 miles - fair is fair - without a definite chance of reunification.

Faaaast forward to today's sojourn to the dark beyond. I very excitedly find a cutting board, some pillow cases and....low and behold......one black effn goddamned Nike swoopy golf shoe........

Well, the quarantined 'hood got an earful and I just about broke my leg getting out of there with the damn box - grumbling, grousing and bitchin all the way.

After disinfecting myself, even though I'm the only one that's been in there since last year, what it really means is the whole shoe thing is definitely my fault. Nobody to share the blame with, argue with ("You should've packed it!! You Know you would've wanted that shoe for golf") Oh shaddup

So now, THIS shoe needs a safe place...you know that place where you put things so you don't forget where they are?? So I don't forget it next time? ....ya....ya....ya....

# CHAPTER 4

## THE KITCHEN......

Good Morning. Come one, come all.. oh wait, no. We can't do that...just pretend we are all having circle time.

Sometimes, over coffee, we all try to plan our day. You know how that goes, get up, stumble to the kitchen (Dolly Parton nailed it in 9-5). So while we're stumbling and getting coffee or tea or the warm beverage of your choice, sometimes the answer to the day's dilemma is right there, in your face. Sometimes, that's because it is a low-hanging power cord from your kitchen ceiling light, which can nearly garrotte you like an after-dark mystery novel whilst you clamour for caffeine, but mostly it's a "wow, I had a good sleep and can now solve the problems of the world" kind of awareness.

This morning, not so much. I have been trying to figure out how to get a few things from storage to "enhance" my living experience here at The Bay. With quarantine on, rental trucks are off. With a near-state of house arrest and the worry of infection for all, I can't ask anyone to get anything of mine...anywhere...

I need Plan B.

As I sip this morning's elixir of life, I begin working out scenarios. Well....I want my kitchen table back in. I look around "Ahah!" I think. But not too loudly, only half a cup in. I spy my suitcases piled in a corner of the living room in the space usually reserved for my tv cabinet, which you may recall from another day, is currently shrink wrapped in the kitchen, right about where the table should go. I could do a switch, I think excitedly. Haul the cabinet into the living room, install the wonderful loaner tv friends so kindly brought to the porch and thus...you don't hear Thus too often, now do you?? So, I could stack the suitcases in the kitchen then put a....hmmmm what could I put on top to make a flat table top......I look wildly around like a woman who just dropped a cookie in a wolf pack. This is shaping up to be either the worst Ahah I've ever had or an invention worthy of a patent. I rummage around in the front of the cottage and find a leaf from the dining room table. I could put the leaf on top of the suitcases and "presto chango" (sometimes we need a change of descriptive text).....The newfangled table begins to take shape in my mind. I could use the old yellow rope in the back room to batten down the hatches, I could tie it off to the much-maligned tv cabinet, I could....

But wait. This is all starting to sound way too much like a really bad Nancy Drew/McGyver type thing. I mean, even for me. As I go back into the front room, the last "I could" is followed by a sigh. I think I just need to fuhgeddaboutit.

I'll just sit here at the dining room table while I think the whole thing through again.

# CHAPTER 5

Welcome back and thanks to those faithful folks who've been following my exploits/adventures in "Camping in Your Own Home" otherwise known as "Where the $&@# is that?"

I mentioned, in a prior offering, the vintage 1928 bed in my room I'm setting up to sleep in. Thus far, I've been camping in the living room on the pullout couch. Some nights I live on the wild side and just sleep on the couch, others I do the full Monty and pull the thing out...comforter, blanket, comforter and a thick layer of track pants and sweatshirt. And socks, only the fuzzy ones...I have a few pair...pairs?? Never sure. Maybe the teacher-types can enlighten me. One of my besties is a teacher type named Pair...I get so confused.....

Anyhow, so I want to get my bedroom ready. Also aforementioned was a lack of sheets. I'm thinking, hell, I'm a tough broad, I can use the comforter/blanket/comforter thing on the bed. But sheets would be so loverly. Low and behold....(right up there with Thus, that one) I find sheets yesterday in my foray to the front of the back shed. I eagerly wash them up, thankful that no winter-hibernating creatures of the country have taken up residence over the long months and get them ready for the bed. Now, this was last night, that I get the brainwave that I want to do this now. 8pm. I've had all day, but no. Dark and gloomy out there..and in here too. I realize, as I so often seem to be doing, that I am missing something. No lamp. I look up. No ceiling light either. No switch on the wall. But where the light should be, there is a plate covering the electrical-thingy (technical term, not for the faint of heart) that Used to be a light. But....no switch. I search high and low. Not on the wall, the closet (microscopic though it is, tucked under the attic stairs) even the floor. So how in the heck did anybody in the last 72 years ever turn on that light????? I shake my head in abject sorrow.

So now, I have a bed, sheets, blanket, comforter all locked in eternal darkness after sunset. Sunrise won't be bad, I think, thinks I, brightness etc. for the oncoming day. But it's that in-between time of black as night because it IS night-time. "A couple of deals before dawn" as those from Guys & Dolls days will recall. Which, if I was younger, would be fine. Find my way anywhere in the dark, the green cat eyes kicking in and never needing to get up in the night. But now....nope.

So my next forage into the cardboard forest had better unearth a lamp or a flashlight or....Ahah! Well, crap, I think. Why didn't I think of this before? Because I've been too busy writing all this $&@* down.

# CHAPTER 6

## LAUNDRY TALES....

Good morning & Happy Sunday to y'all. Before I share today's little bit of camping hell, I just want to reiterate: Stay Home and Wash Your Damn Hands.

PSA for the Day, then. Carry on.

Today's tiny twaddle is a wee story about a lass who flew awa home from afar with nothing but clothes, wine and vodka to her name (or at least in her car). She huffed and she puffed just to prove she could, and once that was done, had to have a nap since that part is so exhausting.

When Cinderella (hereinafter known as Cin) arrived on her doorstep, her larder was empty. Thank god for the aforementioned car...food and supplies were aplenty. Alas, (and alack, lest we forget to recall there was a lack) unbeknownst to Cin, there was one teensy weensy problem. The water worked, things flushed and ran, however, the washing machine refused to join the rest of the appliances in working solidarity. It must've voted against the current regime. Of course, this was not discovered until the larder was full and the car was empty. The plumberguy, already on speed dial, having been summoned to open the castle the prior week, was dialed with haste and alacrity (there's that lack again) and requested to present his learned self a-sap. When he was done with the sap, he was asked to get his arse over here and attend. Unless, of course, there were others in more dire straights than ole Cin, then waiting was fine. All was well in the Kawarthalands and he and his essentials attended, fully and appropriately swathed and covered, as befits a plumberguy during these strange and unknown times, with wipes, gloves, disinfectant and distancing. A minor repair to the clogged water line and a coup d'état was performed, the washer falling somewhat grudgingly in line.

All is not for naught, however, as Cinderella will now have a nice, clean dress to wear to the ball (should one ever be scheduled within the next millennium) maybe one of those hoop dresses everyone thinks would be great right now, along with her choice of 8 pairs of golf shoes or 42 flip flops with matching earrings.

All hail to our essential service workers as they navigate these rough and uncharted waters. May they have good health and our support as they sally forth each day bringing service and assistance to all who need them.

# CHAPTER 7 – PART 1

## TECHNICAL DIFFICULTIES

Happy Monday to you! Hope all are well and coping.

Warm up your cup and let's get to it.

Because I was packing in such an all-fired panic to come home last week, I left my laptop charger there. I know, I know... who does that? Are ya new???? I do that. Have you not been reading these true missives of daily life?!? Have you learned nothing?? I use my phone for most stuff and laptop for some. So these delightful penny dreadfuls you've been receiving for the last few mornings, are being typed on my phone. I brought the laptop, forgot totally about charging the thing. After a weird, unreal drive back from palms to pines, I went to get the laptop going and it was dead. Not "not only merely dead" like a Munchkin, but toast..like it had been in my toaster that's packed somewhere far, far away.

So I can't do the stuff that laptops do. Being socially distanced from everybody and everything, I think, with a famous lightbulb, (sometimes you need to substitute Ahah for something else) I will order one. It's the thing to do. I can't beg, borrow or steal one from anybody right now, I am in the Q, after all and especially since my laptop is from 2011, I'm surprised it still works. I know I can't til I figure this out. So I order the "right" one from Amazon. (Insert praying hands). Here by Thursday, the little site says, just as long as I pay $12.42 for S/H. I'm thinking it would be faster than having my good buddy mail it up here so I've got no choice, so I pay.

Here comes Thursday. I'm madly checking the tracking number so thoughtfully provided by Amazon. Ship by Purolator, should arrive today. Then I start looking through the shipping manifest. See, I know the odd thing, it's the even ones that trip me up like that sump pump pipe in my side yard.

Ship to sorting...Etobicoke.

Ship to distribution...Niagara .....oopsy.

If you know anything about the geography of Ontario, you will know that you do not get to The Bay from the East End of Toronto by way of the Falls. So, add another day and another 00 miles. Update: your shipment is late, you should get it Friday if we don't send it to Kalamazoo, MI first. But they won't because it's not essential, can't cross the border. It's only essential to me and I don't have it yet as they thought it was essential for it to see the the 8th Wonder of the World before it is wonderful enough to charge my laptop. Maybe it had to be charged up first with all that hydroelectric power swishing back and forth across those international waterways. So it arrives Friday, a big OMG, just like the teeny tiny little note says. In its sealed, plastic, been-everywhere-in-Southern Ontario industrial package.

If you want to know how this whole fiasco ends up, tune in tomorrow for CHAPTER 7 - Part and find out the Rrrrest of The Story! ....Paul Harvey would be so proud...

# CHAPTER 7 – PART 2
## TECHNICAL DIFFICULTIES

As I see the truck through the window, I run anxiously to the door, armed with my gloves (old unused dog poop bags) and disinfectant wipes. I wait until the driver is back at the truck before opening the door, to see that he has put the high mileage package between the doors. Not only do my doorknobs now need disinfected but now the inside and outside of my doors. Sigh. Can't be too careful, you never know where it's been (Insert eye roll here). I first pick up the package carrying it around to the back porch. While I'm doing this, I realize I'm going to need scissors to get into the thing because while delivery has finally been deemed essential, adult-friendly pre-antibacterial easy package access has not.

While I'm juggling the package, the wipes and grabbing the scissors, I drop the package. It slides down my sweater and onto the deck. So now I need to disinfect the sweater. Now I'm getting frustrated. I look around. No sweaters handy. How do I find one while not putting the rest of this crap down? I spy an old zip up hanging inside at the door. I decide to wait til I'm done, get it all over with at once. Now picture this, if your imagination isn't fried already: holding the oblong bundle of joy in one hand, it slipping to and fro as poop bags, which gracefully adorn both hands, are sliding off my hands and heading south and I can't get a grip to cut the pouch open. I think, I'm going to cut my hand off and nobody else is here to hear me scream. Finally, I get it all still then I get the plastic bag opened. Yay! Not yay. Discovering there is now a cardboard box inside. Definitely not yay. How do I do this without putting down the scissors because I can't pick them up without loosing my baggies. Well, I decide at that point, to hell with it. I'm trying to keep physically, socially distanced and disinfected but the only thing in the distance right now is my sanity. One handy bag then flies off into the chilly breeze. As I lunge to catch it, it flutters to the ground landing on top of the cut plastic. Useless, and now left holding the right bag with the wrong hand, I finally put my cold free hand into my pocket to warm up. I feel something strange in there. I grab it, bringing it out into the light of day to find it's a pair of old yellow scrubbing gloves from who knows when. In the pocket. While I'm frigging around with crap bags. There really is no good deed that goes unpunished. I throw the other black wee baggie after the first and by a careful balancing act worthy of the great Wallenda, I get the gloves on, the package and scissors re-wiped, dump the cardboard box on top of the disinfected area and disinfect the cardboard. At this point, I figure I won't need the scissors anymore so down they go, with a clatter. Wrong. After dumping the cardboard box out I find my quarry all nicely, hermetically sealed like it's going in the freezer for 6 years. Labelled, dated and everything, no sharpie required. Agghh! By this point, I couldn't care less if I ever plug the damn thing in again, ever. I just want this to be over. Heaving sigh worthy of Jack Benny's Maxwell...look it up...I wipe the scissors yet again, cut the plastic and spill the charger into my other gloved hand. I wipe the whole thing down, pitch everything on the ground and run inside to the laptop. I plug the @&)% cord in and it Works! Great Scott, Batman, who knew?

# CHAPTER 8

## TV AND OTHER ENTERTAINMENT...

Good Morning! Day followed by night, followed by day. Feeling like that right about now. I could use a little hippy dippy, nose pressed to the glass and peering out like I'm the girl in the plastic bubble. My phone says only "1,888km to JDs traffic is light, arrive in 3.5 hours". I guess it knows it's time for oatmeal. Sigh.

Today was miserable out for most of the day. Rain all day but the thermometer looked like it was thinking about white stuff. I'm staring out the window in my latest suave, sleek pair of sweats that still fit during this non-stop bake/cook/eat fest we all seem to be having and I realize my car has been parked for over a week and not been started. I should start it "just in case". In case of what? In case it wants to go somewhere without me? Not a bad idea, thinks the car. Look what happened last time I took her somewhere. We ended up here in the driveway, parked for all eternity because nobody's going anywhere at all. Self isolation is the necessity of our time, right now. Sneak to the gas station all by itself?...no, it's got gas courtesy of Angola NY. The dump? Closed. The Italian deli? No, wait that's down where we just came from and the Pick 3 dinner special might not be considered essential. It's still raining. I start the car with the remote. While it's out there running, I find out, courtesy of social media, that Elton John is doing a concert on TV. I need to hook up those TVs that my friends so kindly dropped off to my porch so I can watch it. I get one tv and the cable box and the cable and tada! Another technical term... It should all work together in peaceful harmony and prime viewing pleasure for years to come, right?

I take the coax, hook it to the back of the tv. Plug in the outlet, jiggle it a bit because you always have to. You're supposed to, it's a rule. Have a hammer ready in case the jiggling doesn't work. I look at the box. There are too many things still empty on there. My car is still running. I need to shut it off. So I realize that it's still pouring rain out there and I'm in here...dry... and not soaked because I ran out to turn off the car. I guess it will have to run the requisite 10 minutes then turn itself off without slinking quietly down the driveway like a fox on silent approach to the hen house because I'm not going out there. Run out of gas, that will teach you!! The car just does a headlight eyeroll Judge Judy would be proud of. Back to the cables. I hook and plug and fasten and attached and Nothing At All. Just like Bonnie Tyler except no yelling. The Box and The Screen…a really bad rock group. Not be gellin', those two. In the meantime, I'm talking on the phone with my marvy neighbour, Janice, who says somebody in the family is heading to town and might be able to get an ethernet cable for me. I suggest we wait, as I'm not exactly sure what all I need. Another neighbour messages and says has a cable, can deliver with groceries in a few days. Well, hot damn, says I, cables coming out of everywhere! So, this still leaves me with Canada…MTV, MuchMusic or CP24. When I turn on my tv with no cable hooked up, I get French Language information, an outdoors channel and CBS How the H. E. double hockey sticks I get CBS is beyond me without getting any reception of the Canuck Big 3 - CBC, CTV, or Global. I look everywhere for Irv Weinstein. Weird internets in the Kawarthalands, as Pluto would say. I see that it is on iHeartRadio so I download that. All good but no video. It is radio, after all. So then I see Fox News is live streaming it all over any of their stations. Can you get that in Canada and make it work? They always say "not offered in your country, so sorry". I never thought I would ever be downloading Fox anything but I wanted to see Elton so I tried it. I couldn't believe it when the news came on and even gave me the option to watch live tv. It worked! I got to watch it with the rest of you, just like a human. But go figure. To watch a Brit on TV in Canada, I have to download an American tv app since none of the hometown options are available.

Carry on, then, stay dry and wash your hands.


# CHAPTER 9A

### CHICKEN CHALLENGED….

Happy April Fool's plus 1. How are y'all out there in Q land? Slug your mug and let's get going. Had something else I was going to share today, hence 9A, however, this seemed more appropriate to the day. Maybe 9B will appear later on, when you least expect it, like everything else that happens here.

I had a chicken challenge when I was away this winter, needed resolution by doctor and outpatient procedure. I know...only me. Now keep your clean hands to yourself and listen up. The aftermath of the adventure required me to see another doctor, get meds and a number of insurance follow ups online and by phone. They were all very thorough and I have nothing but praise and thanks for doctors, healthcare and my insurance, in both countries. Plus, they required an additional scope to be done while I was home in Cold Country Canada in January. That never happened, as I was not deemed urgent enough at that time and the doctor did not have OR time for someone that was fine. That was okay with me...who wants to be that kind of urgent? So it was rescheduled to now. However, "Now" is not now anymore....nor it is likely to be "soon" or even "in the near future". Now is No Scope For You!. Because of this, they scheduled an online video conference with the doctor. I was very impressed that my little food fowl up rated that kind of attention. The doctor came on after 10 minutes (it really was like being there in the waiting room) and explained everything pertaining to my situation and the fact that they are hampered by our current situation. Not much different than January, however, much different reasons. I am, again, quite fine with that. I'm fine, all good and I've even been able to eat chicken again. Slower than the line up at Kawartha Dairy in July but eating it just the same. Case closed...or is it? The doctor went on to say that he would like me to call again in a few months to reschedule the scope and it would all be checked out at that time, depending on the COVID-19 situation and the protocols and needs that are in place then. He would like to determine and confirm there are no underlying health issues (other than I sometimes have been known to eat too fast) and that it will follow the procedure that is normally followed. How could I not agree? A doctor, in the face of all that is going on right now, still wanting to follow up on my wee little episode, made me very thankful for healthcare and for the medical community at large.

Carry on during these troubling times and give thanks to all those on the front lines. Wash your hands, help where you can and thanks for tuning in.

# CHAPTER 9B

## SAGA OF A SPOON...

Thought I'd share this one now as 9A was more serious and sometimes we just need to laugh!

How is everybody doing this morning? Got coffee? Got food? Got wine? Never mind the first two if you have the third.

I've been very blessed with neighbours and friends delivering necessities to my porch during this time of crisis we are all experiencing. Thankful and humbled by the concern folks are showing each other. We might just get through this yet.

Today's corny chronicle is the Saga of a Spoon. If you've been a regular follower of my exploits/dumbass things that seem to happen only to me, you might cast your thoughts and mind back to an earlier tome where I mentioned the hunt for cutlery. I was lucky enough to find some in the abyss that is my shed, however, along with the usual assortment of knives & forks, there was one teeny tiny tea spoon from an earlier millennium. My grandmother would've used one like this for her tea from 1928-1987 and been thankful. I'd be thankful, too, if I just had a few more of them. Along with their sisters in scooping, the table spoons. I keep checking...somehow thinking the shed will cough them up if it doesn't realize I'm actually looking for them and not something else. A garden hoe...(but maybe there's spoons over here beside the shovel). Some pots to match the lids I found the other day (it won't know). Maybe it will think I'm still looking for the other black swoopy golf shoe.... even though I'm sure it's heard the news that there's no golf in the near future and both the shoe and the shed have laughed about this over cocktails.

Spoons. If I were a spoon, where would I be? In a G.D. drawer, like any sane, normal piece of cutlery. With the spatula, holey-spoon and bacon-flipping tongs I can't find either. But there's nothing sane about any of this...I can hear you out there.....you think I can't? Just ask the shed.....

Could I make a bigger spoon? Hmmmm. Possibly. Hey, I could use the tape from the purolator package to fasten The Spoon on a knife, of which I have plenty, and use it to stir and mix and cook all those fattening goodies that seem to be a right of passage through these dark straits. Even the word.... spoon. Soooon a spooooon.

Almost another language. Strives for knives..horks for forks.., nah, not that one.

But surely you can see my dilemma. I can't join the rest of you in accumulation of adiposity if I can't fork it in with my spoon. I will just have to carry on Forkin' til my spoons decide they've laughed long enough at me and miss the rest of their gang at the local spoon saloon. Carry on, then.

# CHAPTER 10

### DAY 14...

Gooood Morning, my cooped up caffeine deprived crew. You must be or you wouldn't be languishing about here waiting for something else to happen to yours truly. Languish no more, my comrades, companions and confidants! Number 10 it is! Day 14 of Q, ten stories for you, let's see if you've learned anything new?

How many spoons do I have? Ha.

How many shoes did I find?.....meh

How much was the shipping and handling on the laptop charger?.....

What colour are today's pajamas?....

hee hee trick question.

How many tv cords do I need?....even I couldn't figure that one out.

Day 14....omg. Looked it from afar, didn't think it would ever get here. But it has arrived, although, now that it's here, it's SSDD. I mean, not much different except now I'll be able to get my own groceries and for the others who've helped me. Woohoo for that! The thing I don't know the answer to is how many times I'm going to go into the shed and look for something. And not find it! I kid you not, the energy today was sorely lacking from other days. I think listening secretly to the car plot and plan ways of escape from the driveway is getting to me. It's been talking to the shed....

Today, I thought I would try a new thing...The Bunkie. For those unfamiliar with cottage country life, often many getaway places have place to getaway from the getaway. A small sleep shed, a corner cube, a tiny house for guests to sleep in, extra company or even for you, when they've all come home for the weekend and you pick the bunkie to hide out in. "Has anybody seen Mom? I don't know, she was here a minute ago"...heh heh...as you slink stealthily across the backyard dragging booze, glass, earplugs and sleeping bag behind you...they'll never find you, you think...and as you turn around to open the door..."Mom....eye-roll...where's the snacks/the dog/the beer/the leftover pizza from last night?". Sigh. They must've seen the earplugs...

When it's fall and you need somewhere to put the extra lawn chairs and a blow up mattress. So some of my erstwhile items from another time ended up in there as well and I thought, well heck, why not look? It's way too cold (I'm a wuss) to go hunting for any length of time but a quick in and out would do. So after I find the right key, I start scrounging in there for anything useful. My key rings would make a Victorian jailor proud. Oh look, Wedding dress from wedding #2...lovely gown, but unless it has spoons in that headpiece, I'm not interested today. Ceramic orange pumpkin for October. Nope. Tassimo coffee....I could take the 85 disks apart and put them all in the drip and make a pot..or 7....sounds like way too much work when I can grind some (thanks, Amz). Of course, I could drag the tassimo machine in there too but really..how many coffee making methods does one person need..melitta one cup drip, coffee pot, the counter is getting full already. I'll save those in case this goes on forever. And ever. Backup coffee. Kinda like the back up bunkie. Good to have stuff in reserve even if it is a small house with big ideas. Oh. A box of hangers. Lovely. If I ever find my closet racks, they would be just dandy. I have a whole small room dedicated to closet space with nothing in it except my two coolers from the big drive. Suitcases are living in the front porch, half full of the clothes they contained as the other half was used for the necessities of confine: wine and vodka! I have to warm the clothes up before I put them on..socks on the heat stove, dungarees in the dryer.....I'm old, ok? And, as previously noted for those possibly older than me and deaf, wussy. For now, since nobody in their right mind would sleep in the bunkie or the porch for the next two months, those hangers can hang out just fine where they are. March is out like a moose with a pine cone stuck in the wrong place. It's not gonna be warm enough anytime soon for bunkie bunking.

Oh lookie, lookie there! A "Life Is Better At The Cottage" sign. Well really. Whoever said that has not obviously lived at MY cottage as of late. It's over there beside the hangers, in the corner, neglected and forlorn.

I guess whoever made that sign has lost their charging cable and hasn't been tuned into recent exploits by the Lake. What In the actual.....hey, I could make up my own sign.

"Abandon Hope All Ye Who Enter Here"

"Go ahead, Find The Spoons, I Double Dare ya!"

"What Happens In The Shed Stays In The Shed"

I'll hang it on the front door.

# CHAPTER 11
### PEST CONTROL...

Get that cup and fill'er up!

Right now, along with my coffee I await the arrival of two guys and a truck. Sadly, they are not young, strapping firemen with puppies. The other day, I while I was putting the finishing touches on the note of the day for the next morning, it was quiet and I was busy writing away when I thought I heard a funny noise. I listen but don't hear anything. I carry on, only to hear it again. This seemingly endless supply of Do Nothing Days has my mind wandering and making stuff up where it wasn't before. You're reading this, aren't you? Where is it coming from? In the old days, I would've said my pencil on the page but I was typing. Laptops with cords don't make those sounds. There it is again. I look up, over, around. Nothing. As I try to figure out if the stove is acting up, or I'm hearing a random goose outside just returning from the south and arguing about being quarantined, I hear it again. Only this time, it's really loud and in the kitchen. Wrong stove. But, it doesn't sound like a stove. I don't know what it sounds like but I don't think I want to know. Maybe I could just hang up a sign and carry on with my day.

Next thing, I hear it in the hall. I go out there, wishing I had a canoe paddle or 1.75L of vodka handy as a weapon but I would have to abandon my post and I might lose the sound. There it is again, only this time, it's above me. I look up, waaaay up. I don't see the Friendly Giant but I do hear what sounds like a small sasquatch running in the attic. Of all the things, so close to the day of liberation, I have to hear new upstairs neighbours moving in. I can't quite believe it, I think with a wail. The car and the shed are behind it. I know it!

Scrabbling in the walls and ceiling at this time of year can mean several things. Squirrels, mice or raccoons. Country living at its finest Probably other things I don't know about, too. Sigh. Too heavy to be mice. Usually raccoons are nocturnal so this being afternoon, I didn't think so. So, leaves me with Door #3, Monty. Squirrels. Those buggers are not the cute, furry friends with a nut-filled mouth we see in the picture books. These can cause damage, invade in ones or twos and leave an awful mess behind when you finally catch them.

I start getting a wee little bit uptight. Start? Who am I kidding? Getting upset progressing rapidly to holy crap, what next? Do not want this right now. Of course, there is no good time for it to happen but, seriously. Has enough not happened already in two short weeks? I'd get in my ever-grumbling car and head back from whence I came, if I could.

While I listen to the shuffling up there, I decide they are dancing and wishing it was happy hour. I don't hear any singing so it must not be a good band. I wish I was dancing at happy hour. Vodka, music, friends. This whole thing could be blotted out, glossed over and hidden in the bunkie for just a little while. Deny, deny, deny! I decide I'd better put down the virtual vodka before I get a real one and check things out further. I look around and can't see anything looking like invasion of the body dancing squirrels. So I go outside. I walk all around the house, peering and peeking but don't find anything til I get to the far side. It's always the far side, this stuff never happens on the near side, or right here or oh look at that, and in plain sight, too, how thoughtful. No way. You never get to just go look and solve the problem. At least, I never do. I find an opening in the crawl space big enough to pour coal down 80 years ago. Oh my god. Anything could've got in through that. It had been sealed up. Ugh!!!! So with that, I'm looking up pest guys and calling numbers. I leave a message with one and talk to two more. In the meantime, I don't want to go back in. I'm hoping it'll come out, see me and head for the hills or the lake, anywhere but here. Doesn't happen. So I'm standing outside when I find out two Sasquatch Sheriffs aren't in my area and the third will call me back next morning and confirm. Double ugh.

So I'm left with a squirrel ( I hope) that will stay where it belongs, out there while I'm in here. All is well, the Sheriffs ride up when they're supposed to and it gets sealed up, saying the dance party can get out but not back in. Perfect. All the while, all I can think of is even a damn squirrel is getting out before I do.

# CHAPTER 12

## PLEASE, RELEASE ME!

Morning Everybody! How do you like your coffee? Done, so you can run out the door!

Omg omg omg !!!! "Please release me...let me go" my new favourite song! Engelbert has nothing to fear, however. It has been reached, ladies and germs..but germs are bad so wash your hands before you read any further. As I sit here warming my hands around my cup and my socks on the stove, .don't judge... all I can think is I can go, I can go, I can go....The car has been practicing stealth manoeuvres in the driveway, engine on silent skedaddle, able to leap tall potholes in a single bound. This is the Bay, land of unfixed roadwork and 30,000 leagues under the puddle...you hit any of that, we won't see you til next golf season, especially sad since we would still like to see you sometime this golf season. If there is one.

So many ideas, so little radius. Here..there...then go home. So where in my here and there can I go? I really-really-really want my guitar. It would help in these times of strife and sorrow. I could write a new hurtin' song. Look out, Hank Williams. Oh my god... I could play it backwards and all my missing crap would come back! I ponder this, quickly discarding. I might not be able to be selective....I would love a couple of extra things from the grocery store. I can pick up a few things for A&A, who have had custody of said items all winter. The cables for the tv...I'll grab the tv as well, it's with the guitar. They are plotting a bad song then they'll broadcast it!! They are in cahoots with the swoopy black shoe. That's what I'll do. I'm so excited. My coffee done, socks are warm and off I go.

I manage to wiggle waggle my 4 wheeled jalopy down the rutted lane that passes for a county road and arrive at....gasp...The Highway. Sharp intake of breath, sudden attack of the vapours, temporary blindness sets in at the magnitude of it all....Now What? Left turn - gas & chips. The car is pulling left. Don't need gas, already have gas from eating too many chips. Tank is nearly full, haven't gone anywhere. The car is muttering, not my fault....

I decide Left as the guitar and tv cables are that way. OMG, not sure I can handle it. I Can Go Out..I cannot believe it. Not the little out – out to the porch, the shed, well, maybe not the shed. Sitting here at the corner of Chips and Freedom and I don't know where to go or what to do. And I've been waiting sooo long. I could almost cry. I have food, as a number of folks have kindly brought me whatever I've needed these last two weeks, so I don't need anything. The abject sorrow in saying that. Thousands would do a big pouty and be green like my grass after the sump pump runs for two hours. So what do I almost sort of need...besides out of here. We aren't supposed to go out unnecessarily so I rack what's left of my brain in an effort to come up with something I can go get that I can almost really need.

But, wait...says Dudley Do-Right. Nell, it ain't quite that easy....

I need to see the kids. Can't do that. Social distancing and workday. Have to continue online. Girlfriends, same. No peopling. Local dump. Again, closed like my favourite bars. Spoons and red pajamas? I know!!! WINE!!!! There it is...phew. Thought of something. I feel so much better already. I know that it's busy in town at some of the stores and many things that used to be on the shelves are AWOL right now so do I want to take the chance and go all the way in there and be SOL? I know a place that's the other way. The Left way. The car snickers as I slowly I turn left. I make my way, picking up speed as I get more confidence behind the wheel. It's been awhile, you know. Time to turn right then left to get to Chips & Gas. Gas? nah. All good. Wait a damn minute. 66c. Holy crap, hasn't been 66c/litre since I drove a Pinto. Slight right and $20.00 gas is mine!!!! Wow. I could get to like this. Tap, wipe and outta there. Of course, now that gas is finally affordable, we can't go anywhere.

Along from Gas is lovely little country store that is also an Agency store. For wine and liquor, for those unfamiliar with the term. I sidle alongside the building, waiting for the other car to leave before I get out. I'm new at this, don't want to do it wrong and be yelled at first time out of captivity. But It's all good. Inside, two folks are keeping distant and doing their deals. I find a small bottle of Kim Crawford for $9.00. That's a half. Three more of those left on the shelf. I could have two whole bottles if I bought them all. Wowee. I could share them with the squirrel. Pickings are slim, indeed. I also get chips, to shut the car up. After the counter is wiped, the machine is tapped and the bill is printing, I'm given a squirt of sanitizer. Pretty awesome, I think!

From here, I carry on to groceries in the wee hamlet over yonder. I arrive, breathless with derring do. I can do this. Armed with phone, list and wipes, I sally forth. After following the route, it's like lining up for "It's A Small World " at Disney...back and forth, follow the yellow brick road. Check out-Oz. When I get to Oz, the Wizard is behind the plexiglass curtain and I say I want all three. She looks at me like I'm nuts (☺) and continues to ring it all up. Swipe, wipe & load. Kinda like stop, drop & roll without the nuclear event. Delivery of same, also a breeze! Tv, guitar etc. awaits in garage, leave groceries, wave and yell and ooh ahh John Travolta, ooh ahh back inside.

I got stuff, my stuff, all by my oneliest self! What a great feeling. And I helped out family. All good. And all safe. I feel so good, now we're gonna song. Everybody, in your best Bette Midler. "From a Distance"!

# CHAPTER 13

## WARDENS OF WILDLIFE...

Lucky 13. Huh. Today's little love letter harkens back to the invasion of the nosy, body snatching squirrels. After extensive discussion and collaboration the other day, a one-way door was installed so the little bastards could leave and not be able to come back in. The Wardens of Wildlife assured me that this method of "extraction" is fail safe and fool proof, however, they neglected to send the memo to the wily beasties. Late last night, whilst putting away the guitar and assorted flotsam and jetsam around here, still floating on my great escape day, I heard a noise.....a really big noise, the biggest, hugest noise there ever was. In the wall, down the hall, in the ceiling, crap I'm reeling.... not Again!! This time, when I banged the wall it scrabbled and ran up into the kitchen ceiling. I guess it's saving the living room for later. Oh joy.

This was not going to go well. A long, tiring night ensued. I called the purveyors of pesty problems first thing and they agreed, a problem was occurring. Normal pesky pests usually depart from the interior to find food, then return later only to find a roadblock and the border closed to all non-essential traffic. In this case, however, not so much. The damn thing not only didn't leave, it sounded like it was building a condo in my attic with every piece of construction equipment going. The good guys did more investigating and announced that it was most likely not a squirrel or even a few or a bunch. It was probably a raccoon and

because the exit door was too small, it burrowed in and is most likely a pregnant female making a nest.

Well, gag me with a spoon. A preggo pesky pest. Just what nobody needs in their attic, in addition to the bats already alive and well in my belfry. I can't believe it. Who did I tick off in the universe? I can't even blame it on the shed. I can't figure out why nobody else has mentioned it in the neighborhood. Of course, they'd have to shout it at me from their yard, from a socially distant six feet away and " hey, I got critters in my attic" is not something you're going to yell for all and sundry to hear. Besides, they've probably got little squirrels, if they have anything, not big pregnant mama raccoons. It's a good thing mandatory quarantine didn't last longer, I'd probably be inviting it in for tea and knitting a hat and booties.

So the nice guy installed a bigger exit and said he'd be back tomorrow to find out what's going on. He would also like a report, if it's not too much trouble, on comings and goings and any and all noise worthy events. So now, I'm on raccoon patrol. Late night varmint vigil to report any nocturnal rumblings in the up above. Eye roll. Somebody bring the popcorn.

# CHAPTER 14

## VARMINT VIGIL...

Good Morning, Peeps and Peepettes!

Put down your cup, turn your hearing aids up and gather around the old Corningware perk while I share the latest not greatest chaff for a laugh. Coming to you live from NNN, the No Nonsense Network aka All True, nearly most of the Time! Gather around, my pretties, as I provide the latest in indoor/outdoor breaking (or maybe just slightly cracked) news. I do have a Corningware pot, by the way...the more shocking part is I know where it is. The spoon is pointing at the car with just a hint of "Huh. I told you so" with a bit of glistening on the bowl. It could be a tear...

The latest on the creeping creature of the cottage wall...nothing. No sound since last report. No noise, no mutter, no rattle, crash or boom. I'm almost disappointed. I had hoped the smarmy illegal would slink out of the new egress with at least of modicum of shame, into the yard and go haunt everybody else.

So tonight, I'm on varmint vigil, once again. And of course, I keep hearing things. Live or playing in the constant movie going on in my head. I think it's a cartoon. The bang and thump of the stoves going on. The hum of the water pump And my ever present good buddy, imagination, getting more and more tuned into the situation as it cooks up stuff far worse than anything I've written yet. I need really good theme music now. A bump? It's moving and coming through the ceiling any second. The sump pump comes on? Apocalypse armageddon. An actual real life creature cacophony? Nothing. Doesn't the thing have to eat sometime? I know when I was parturient..look it up..mastication was second only to disgorge. The beast needs to eat. But nada. Could it already have left the delightful confines of my penthouse? Hmmm. New mesh, vanished varmint? I have been in here all last night and most of the day and all tonight and not another peep or squawk have I heard. Just for a real time update, it's currently 4:47am this morning and I have, of course, been awake off and on all night and your weather is dark followed by light.

The mind boggles. Is the guy going to come back, take the stuff away and say, "Sorry, ma'am," as he tips his cap at the crazy white haired lady, "I guess we were wrong, weren't we now?" Don't tell the shed.

I'm not sure what the next step is for this one but I do know that it if it's still in there, it better start paying rent. The cost of keeping it in the style to which it's become accustomed is approaching Go Fund Me status and the least it could do is cook the odd meal or bring wine for the next happy hour, white, preferred. I know it's practicing social distancing at its finest but since we seem to be isolated together, dropping it on the porch would be acceptable.

# CHAPTER 15

## TELEVISION – NOT FOR THE FAINT OF HEART

Welcome, my fellow Hot Cups, hope you're happily libated with the bevvy of your choice. I think tomorrow should be Mimosa Hump Day. Of course, if everyone has some champagne and OJ, that would work. Or whatever morning happy breakfast drink that you like to toast with. Baileys in the Java. I'm good with anything that shows up. Hey, if we're all here and awake, all the better! I'm thinking in these times of what the heck day is it anyway, we also probably don't know the time. I know I had red pjs..does that count? I could get the squircoon (my new name for the creature that dwells within) to join us and baby could make three...😺.

Some mornings are Mary Hartman days, you know? Remember her? Slightly stunned woman in a pinafore played by Louise Lasser. Very bizarre things happened around her and she was often at a loss to cope. Hmm. Might have to change my name and get a pinafore. I think sometimes sanity is overrated. Look at what's happening around us now. I think we've all got some Mary Hartman happening. The state of the world at large along with our own worlds and what's happening within. Or not happening. And all from our couch, in our tracksuits. I like to change out the pjs from time to time, just to keep it interesting. That way the neighbours that walk by and wave like those blowup guys on the corner in the wind won't think I never change as I wave back like a maniac on hot coals. The baby likes it....the car sits silently in judgement. Good thing the news crews aren't out there for a tv remote, they'd be doing a story on psychological effects of cabin fever in a partially furnished cabin.

Televisions. I had a great time setting up my tv, said nobody, ever. Tv's, cable, internet, all of these are the big black hole in the living room. Stuff goes on in there and never comes back out. Kind of like my attic. I look at the tv and I look at the box, the wires, cables and cords and long for mom and dad's old Marconi b&w from the basement. Turn it on, done. Maybe wiggle the rabbit ears but you were good. Remember ole Irv? Yup. 11:00pm. You tune it in. That, and the hockey game. If something went on the "fritz" during the hockey game or the Ed Sullivan show, you were scuppered. I never did know who Fritz was or why he always got blamed for television malfunction the world over, but there you have it. Even turning the big dial on the monster size box on the coffee table to turn the antenna to "tune it in better" after the rabbits got their ears back, was fraught with accuracy issues. Stop turning, you went too far. Just a bit more left...hold it!! Perfect. Meanwhile, if you took your hand off it for one second, fuzzy snow screen ensued and you had to start again. Or, you'd be there holding it in place for the entire Mutual of Omaha Wild Kingdom. Long hour of tigers and other wildlife prancing across the screen with you looking sideways so you could hold the button in just right. Later, we had one of the first colour tv's on the block as my dad worked for Motorola and would bring them home to test. The neighbourhood was in our living room in 1972 watching Paul Henderson score his epic goal. In colour.

My tv today has no button, dial or ears. Just a spaghetti of cords and plug in ends that left me clueless.

You know how the cable people say, oh we are so glad you called and we'll put on hold for quite awhile before we get back to you to help you? I was very happy that my supercablegirl (SCG) called me back and was able to help me get things set up in less than the usual two days of strife. Of course, nothing ever happens right the first time or even the second. Or maybe third. This is me we're talking about. Sometimes it takes even longer.

Me. Hello, I have a such n such tv to hook up.

SCG. Hello, Mrs Daimler, I can help you with that

Me. A Daimler is a car, like in Agatha Christie novels and rich peoples driveways and I'm Dahmer, like the serial killer guy.

Why is that always met with silence?

Super, says I.

After three phone calls, two hours, some cords replugged and additional coax cable added, some secret codes punched in, it worked! Not for the techno faint of heart.

I can now watch more than the big three stations I got before. Yippee skippee! The 11:15am PM Update on 7 channels, in two languages, instead of all in French on TVO. Or something.

Tv has always been a good source of entertainment.

# CHAPTER 16

## CAWFEE AND COOKING...

Morning, fellow Isolates! Got that Baileys? The Mimosa?? I would suggest everybody download the "Houseparty" App and let's get this party started. I think I need one this morning. Late night last night....

When I lay me down to sleep,

the sump pump it did start down deep.

On and on it pumped that water,

making it so hard to slumber.

Finally, it came to slowin,

But not before the Melatonin. Sigh.

A slow sleep night in the Kawarthalands. Morning coffee. I think we can make it work. Houseparty is a free App in the App Store for whatever system you use. Most seem to be up and about by 8-8:30. What say we try it around 8:30am for whoever would like to join. Houseparty. PJ's welcome! I can show you my one spoon. I'll even invite the Shed....

Some days, you just want company to share a coffee with. Some days, beautiful, silent isolation is your only wish. Although lately......not seeing so much of that, even from the self-professed self isolationists who made this popular long before our current situation.

I am thinking that in order to get through the thing and, of course, a side dish of solving the world's problems, that either caffeine or alcohol would provide a source for solutions or a welcome distraction. I am thinking we would need tall ones for the current thing. An antidote, if you will. A veritable cornucopia of cope...a plethora of platitudes, a panacea of purpose....a pile of *&%#....

I had heard that the liquor stores here might close before we made the big drive. Thankfully, that hasn't happened. I have some wine, a bit of vodka, some Bailey's, some carmel vodka, some..did I mention I have vodka? All I need is more diet tonic to accompany it and I'll be just FINE. A messenger/facetime/houseparty happy hour and I'll be good!! Might need even more vodka by the end of that....

I'm thinking that some of us are feeling cooped up a bit....the strain.... so besides a desperate hankering for happy hour, I'm thinking I need to tell you about cooking in isolation here. I have a stove, fridge, microwave, just to share that I'm not a complete cave person luddite here, however, I'm lacking a little of the extras. Besides spoons. I have a saucepan, but no lid. An electric frying pan but no cord. A dutch oven with no chocolate......In short, I got some of the stuff but not all of the stuff. And the stuff I do have, I only have some of. Take the pot thing. A medium sized saucepan, you can make K-Dinner, now there's even Dijon ketchup for it, perfect. Put the lid on to drain....not so much. Oh, but wait, there might be a colander hanging on the pot hooks...ok, phew..there is. So next time I'm making that, I can drain the water off. So the electric pan. Love to fry ground beef/onions/garlic etc. in there then add the sauce or soup or noodles or whatever is going in. In this case, nothing is going in since there's no cord. Whatever flippin' box that's in, I have no idea. That damn shed.....it could be a side-deek by the bunkie, will have to check under the bottom mattress beside the zero gravity chair. So, no cord. I could try the huge Rachel Ray fry pan, great size but I've had it so long, the big black flakes that go into the meal can be classed as extra protein. Not for those cooking cream of mushroom soup and pork chops, if you get my drift.

Since I have a wooden spoon and I found a flipper on yesterday's undaunted undertaking into the hinterlands, I can do a modicum of culinary creation. Ground beef, it is, with a couple of cups of Paul Newman's "imported" Roasted Garlic Pasta Sauce and Ta Da! I'd import Paul Newman anytime, really. Dinner, lunch, the aforementioned happy hour...could be a new treat! Of course, he has long since left us to our own culinary devices so I'll have to just dream about it all, but I'd love to even have a virtual visit. Hey, maybe I could call the raccoon Paul Newman....raccoons have blue/green eyes that reflect...that could work..although I'm not sure I'd want to have the thing in for dinner. It's already in...I think. In these times of social distance, I'd be happy if he could eat outside and we'll just wave to each other.

Too much vodka, ya think?

# CHAPTER 17

## ADVENTURES IN SHOPPING...

Good morning! Got your java? Let's jive.

Today's wee wail of woe comes to you courtesy of the letters O,M & G and by the numbers 00 and 85. Dollars, that is...set a spell, kick your shoes off, well, maybe not, it's chilly here. So 00 and 85 became pals the other day in the trunk of the grumbly car. I ventured out into the increasingly creepy world where you're met with all manner of strangely garbed folk all freezing outside 6 feet apart (1.829 meters for any Canuck under 50) waiting patiently like a well-ordered pack of zombies. Fifty years we've been constantly, automatically converting everything back to imperial measurement. Didn't realize it was that long. Tiring, when you think of it. And the secret relief felt when you cross the border and convert your car "back" to Imperial. Well, there was no secret relief yesterday. I waited my turn with everyone else and got sanitized, a sanitized cart and saw just about everyone respecting the rules. Eerie feeling in the store. Full carts and partially empty shelves, like last time, staff making sure they were keeping well away as they stacked, moved and replenished. I move along the arrows, getting the things on my list and for a friend and my daughter. Door dropping is a new pastime. Suddenly, from one of the zombies I hear "Hi Heather" I look wildly around. Which one was it?? They all look the same...agh! I don't know where to look or who to answer! I look up for a wide shaft of light waiting to beam me up. I discover, finally, after standing there like a fool that it's a friend (yes, I have some) and I haven't seen her in awhile. Who has seen anybody? Everyone is covered up or at home. After quick greetings and updates, we carry on, our increasingly loaded carts becoming harder to push through the aisles. Does anybody else do this? I saw coffee on sale. I like coffee. I have some. But, I think, maybe I need just a little bit more, like the Grinch, just in case. As noted in an earlier tome, in case of what? In case I run out? Not likely, I even have backup coffee. And I got some more. But you never know how long this will last and they might not have coffee next time. I might not need it next time, either, but that's irrelevant. So I get some. The kids might need some. Cans of soup. I have about eight already. But I decide I need four more. I don't eat a lot of soup but it's comfort food. And pea soup, the French kind. Yum. Am I the only one calmly purchasing extra staples "just in case"? This is how 00 and 85 became pals in the trunk. Coffee, soup, extra meat. Again, anybody with the meat? I know they'll have some in the stores but I might not always have some...not sure how this will unfold over the duration. I have a turkey, a ham and a chicken already frozen and I live by myself. A whole 9.027 kg of turkey, that's 19.86 lbs to the unmetricated. A new word. Gawd, I could open a restaurant along with a bar, because we could all use happy hour, but I'd have no staff. And only take out, but by then I'll be wanting everybody to take things out..I'll have too much to store. I think I already have enough food for this apocalypse and the next one. Do I need more coffee or is it time to switch to vodka?

I hope the plague of locusts are hungry.

# CHAPTER 18

### REBEL KITCHEN...

Hey there. A groggy am to y'all. Is everybody having trouble sleeping or am I the only one? I figure it's because I have half an ear open for Paul Newman but it's also a sign of stress. I still can't find my loaf pans. I want to make that beer bread I saw that somebody posted. Looks like very few ingredients and easy cooking. Of course, it means wild abandonment of any semblance of dietary restraint but does anyone care right now? Those loaf pans are haunting me. It could require another soirée into shed land. I bundle up and out I go. If I'm not back before the locusts get here, it's been real. Let me see...a box of old photos. Nope, no loaf pans in there. A container of the little metal figures you used to get with tea...not the Tetley tea folk but another kind. My mom had a whack of them, plus two shelves for them. And they're all here. Every one. Not hiding any loaf pans in there, though are ya? See if I find a wall for you. Beside the saw blade in the porch where you'll freeze in spring and fall. Another box, this one has a three level steamer. Oh saints be praised, it is Easter, after all. I can steam all the meat I bought but I can't make beer bread for Easter til I find the dang pans. Are they in box number three? Nope. This one has "kitchen linen". Holy cow, I can finally have more than one tea towel at a time!! I can use one for the bathroom. A lovely red and white striped tea towel in my pink bathroom. Perfect. At least I'll be able to put that one in the wash and use the gold and green one and pretend it's Christmas and not Easter. It looks like Christmas out there right now.

Box number four. I can hardly wait. If you're still reading this, I bet you can't either. A pie plate, an 8x8 cake pan...woohoo..getting closer, a corkscrew and.....an extension cord. Don't ask, I can't tell you. No friggin idea. But no loaf pans.

The next box, ladies and gents, contains a sign that says "happiness is found in the journey not at the destination". Hahahahaha.

I think the pans are having a whale of a time with the spoons. They are starting their own band, it's called Rebel Kitchen and they are going to take it on the road when we are released. Their first gig will be out back in the yard with the shed playing backup. Maybe they'll make some bread.

# CHAPTER 19

## THE PORCH...

Hello and Happy Easter to everyone out there in Stay in Land. Sounds like one of the lands at Disney. Tomorrowland, Adventureland. Iceland, no that's already taken. I think that's here. Hope you're hunkering in and that you need extra moisturizer from all the hand washing. Turkey Day! Coffee up, feet up, listen up! Today's wail of woe comes to you from the front porch. I have a lovely big front porch. An Inside/outside porch. The inside one is only fit, temperature wise, to be an extra fridge right now. Good for leftover turkey storage but too chilly yet for sleeping and sitting in. The outdoor porch is too small to be much more than a place for purolator to deliver things to and sitting watching the sunset. In your snowsuit. The ice is off the bay now and I think it found its way into the porch while it freezes the liner on the big bed and makes the dresser drawers squeak and groan every time I try to pull one out.

A porch is a lovely thing. It overlooks the lake and is also rodent free. Paul Newman won't be watching the sunset anytime soon. I also have this huge saw blade on the wall, yes, a saw blade....a relic of the lands' history as a sawmill in the 1800- early 1900s. Logs were floated down the lake to be milled here and sent on elsewhere for finishing. I have long wanted to renovate the porch into a nicer spot, but it wouldn't be the same without the 486 beer coasters that line the walls. The former owner collected them. "Leafs Win Stanley Cup". Socially distant since 1967. Brador....They've been there awhile. Hey, it would help for when I open that bar. I could use the bed for when folks pass out. We need one out here, a bar, not a bed, silly, since the closest happy hour place is 17km away. It just won't do. I could use the teeny tiny front porch for the singer and the yard for dancing.

Picture this, if you will...beer taps under the saw blade, just grab a coaster off the wall. A take out window for the beer and peanuts beside the little porch so you don't have to miss the music. You could open the drapes to "let the sun shine in". I hear you singing it..don't lie to me.

So if I had a bar, I would definitely need to find the spoons. And possibly the straws, but not disposables. Reusables. Take them home with you, I'll buy more. Surely, the straw manufacturers want to stay in business. So metal straws. And metal toothpicks, for the fruit and the rest of the harvest that can sometimes don a drink. Drinks will cost 9 bucks. Just to cover the price of the straws and toothpicks. It's my fantasy, leave me alone. Who wouldn't want a bar on their front porch? Instant friends! Instant party! Instant neighbours all moving away. Oh, wait, that part isn't good. The neighbours are good here.

They are the best, actually. All of them. Keep an eye on my place when I'm not here and look out for me when I am. We all need that. This afternoon, after my ramble about loaf pans, there was a knock at the door and waiting for me were loaf pans...I never laughed so hard! Thank you so very much, J&F! So, as was noted in a comment in yesterday's post, I would have to make the bread and take one over. And I did, door dropped a loaf of beer bread. If times were different, we would've skipped the barley and gone right to the chilled glasses instead of the hot hops. Not sure how theirs turned out, I think mine was very dense. I *can* hear you thinking, you know. It was actually pretty good, although I think a tiny piece at a time would be enough.

Even the car was hinting for a bite...forget it. Not fit for such a treat. Your tires are fat enough and you haven't had a shampoo since we got home.

# CHAPTER 20

## TURKEY TALE…

Happy Monday morning coffee klatch to y'all. Hope Easter was as nice as it could be and that you were able to socialize distantly between hand washes.

Anybody else spend most of the day online then part of the night when you can't sleep, checking social media, reading, playing games? I find it hard to get into a deep sleep and stay there. Of course, maybe not everyone has half an ear cocked for the latest and greatest from the attic and walls. I'm thinking I need more to entertain me……..

For your morning miasma of minuscule minutiae, I must tell you a turkey tale. You may recall I have an Easter turkey to cook. I very dutifully have been thawing it in the fridge for the requisite four days for a 20 pounder. I followed all instructions and directions as I often get a fresh one so I needed a refresher in preparing one from frozen. I was very thankful to even have a turkey to cook. I've been checking it all the way along and it was coming along nicely and I was quite looking forward to cooking it and sharing it with fellow pandemic prisoners. I got it out, got the pan organized (I had one, who knew?) and got ready to clean/stuff/season. I got the water running to take out the guts and clean the inside and…..Nope. I could not get the plastic doohickey off the leg thing that held it all together. I pulled, shoved and yanked, there was no way that thing was coming off. The cold water is still running. As I got a good grip on it and pulled, I realized what was holding it in place was a piece of ice. I tried to manoeuvre it out and it wouldn't budge. I banged it on the sink bottom, I gouged it with a knife, I pulled the legs. That sucker was still frozen inside, much like my hands, by this point. I could not get a grip on any part of it to get anything out or rinse it through. I couldn't feel if I got a grip anyway, my hands were frozen more solid than the bird. Huge sigh. I try valiantly to get it to loosen it's grip on it's guts. Nothing doing. I finally decide to phone a friend since I can't ask the audience. I call my Chef-in-Chief, Victor Dahling, who advises me to run warm, not hot, water over and through the bird and it will do the trick. Thank god, I say, since I wouldn't be able to run anything anywhere with these frozen hands if I had to keep doing it the way I had been.

Meanwhile, I'm thinking of the folks I was going to door drop dinner to. (dashing to the door having already been taken by Santa and mobile take out food.) Easter is going to be late this year, since the turkey has not risen nor has it even suggested getting up for dinner. It must still be enjoying PJ's and bon bons.

Finally, after much cajoling, coercing and coaxing, the bird gives up the guts and I can yank it all out, get it cleaned and get the feeling back into my frozen fingers. Once it's ready, I stuff it, thinking all the while that stuffing is overrated, as I make even more of a mess making that happen. In the oven it goes, with 4.5 hours on the timer to cook, however, I'm thinking Sunday tee times will be later, allowing for possible frost delay.

Just as it goes in, the timer set, the oven door closed, I hear something. Something not unlike something i've heard before. A noise and not a beautiful one. Rattle, scrabble, thump bang. In the kitchen wall....then in the attic. How do they know??? I look upward in abject sorrow. Unless Peter Cottontail missed his cue, he's up there having coffee and eggs with Paul Newman. Damn. Now they're going to want dinner and it won't be ready. I seriously cannot believe this is happening. I think of who I can call. The only ones I can't call today are the pest guys. Not open. I thought they were essential. Even the damn Easter Bunny was declared essential. They'd better get over here and get him and his non-essential buddy out of my attic.

# CHAPTER 21
## ANIMAL EXPLOITS...

Good morning! Get your cup loaded up! Today's tale du jour finishes with one animal and starts with another. For those who asked, I did get turkey, however, later in the evening but by the time you cook, clean, carve, and cover, consume is far down the menu. Not sure if everyone is the same, I know I'm like that. I thoroughly enjoyed it today, though. There was no further rumpus from the roof, thank god, so all is quiet on the northern front at the moment. I can only hope escape of both Peter and Paul occurred before Mary found out they were missing and came to look. Maybe if she hummed a few bars....

There being a developing storm today, I was advised not to door drop any packages so I didn't. I got a few things done here, plus the daily increase in screen time "you are up 135% from last week" checking in, out and generally "visiting" everyone online that was there. Good time to keep in touch with folks. FaceTime, Messenger and Houseparty are like old friends and it's always good to see whose around.

I also headed to town which I'll tell you about in a minute.

I decided a more concerted approach on my part, was needed to combat the issues I've been having here in my partly empty house. I've been thinking about this for a bit and hadn't finalized anything but today was the day. I needed some help with all that's been going on around me. Sometimes, you just feel that way. Especially with all the changes in our world lately. Makes you feel somewhat vulnerable. Even with /3 of a rock band playing about in your attic, you sure can't count on them for anything except more issues.

I needed somebody who could help chase away those rascally rodents and also be somebody warm who might want to snuggle up at night. Since Sam Elliott is otherwise occupied, I'd like to introduce the newest member of my family. His name is "Seven". So far, he doesn't have a formal name, if he ever did. He's a Walker Hound from the local Humane Society and he's a sweetie. We will be spending the next while getting to know each other and learning what Sit, Stay, and No mean. We already know what Down means because he was a hunting dog and he drops flat when you say the words. He has made great progress with Sit already. Will work for treats. He is affectionate and loves pets and belly rubs. We also need to learn what "want to go outside?" means but that will come, too. As far as they know, he never lived in a house so he is enthralled with the floor, the window and the dog blanket. Might be a wee bit big for a couch potato but the blanket on the floor seems to be quite fine and in one afternoon, he's getting familiar with things and loves the yard. I think he's going to be just fine. Maybe if anybody has an idea for a name, you could share that. Look out, upstairs, you ain't seen nothin yet! 007 is on the job.

# CHAPTER 21

## FIRST NIGHT...

Hello out there, we're on the air it's Hockey Night tonight! Well, not really but it's cold enough to be thinking hockey. Just need to lace 'em up and I'm good to go. The big ice rink in front has melted away but I can make do with the frozen puddles on the driveway. The latest and greatest in your Lakefront News.

I must share with you the exploits of Number Seven's first night. 007 was on the job! A couple of incidents in the afternoon with dogs having a meet and greet from the yard and the bridge over the ditch. Then police presence in our little burg..three cruisers, one parked in front of my house. Don't know who or what they were after but I felt protected, albeit a bit unsettled. Honest, I don't know what I did this time. Not sure there was enough social distancing from the ditch maybe....Seriously, our secret agent canine was a really good dog. And no noise from the heavens. Phew. He loved his blankie, lay on the floor beside the precious window and slept. A bit of wandering around am but I think he was just checking things out. Very happy to sleep and rest, I think. Made sure mama was still there and went back to sleep.

The fun began this morning. Took him out for the first trip around 6:30. He had done so well. All good out there, everything came out alright etc. Came in and I waited til about 7:30 to feed him. Sometimes things can come out faster than they go in. Then to breakfast. We had coffee, chatted, discussed our plans for the day, etc. I got ready to take him out and he wasn't at the door. I go looking. He's decided we should have a second bathroom in the dining room. Last night, he made the same message clear. Sadly, during this time of Q, a second loo is not happening. Even for dudes that have lived outside. I go in there and find, to my shock, two great leaning towers of pooza, bigger than even buddy Bones down south. Boy, the in and out factor here is moving pretty quickly. I don't think he even tasted his breakfast. So I grab the bags, getting one scooped then as I put

that down to grab the other, he takes off with it. Oh my gaaawwd!! I quickly scoop the other pile and chase after him, hollering all the way. I reach the back door and there he is, looking for all the world like a little angel. He's put the bag down and is sitting there, looking up at me grinning with "WTH you worried about, mom, I got this" written all over his face. Oh my god, I just about died. I laughed so hard I could hardly get my coat on and the leash hooked up.

Lots of visits to the backyard and some good walks. There was a bit of "Wtf" when the sumptuous pump went off around 3:00pm. Until then, very quiet. Not quite sure what to make of something else that pees into the yard, are you?

The rest of the day saw a new bed and harness arrive for his highness to sleep and walk with. He seems happy with both. The harness is highly underrated. If you've got a four legged with the strength of eight, you need a harness. Saved my arm. He's responding really well to everything going on, along with some reassurance here and there. I think we will be just fine. What is not fine is the three inches of snow and icy cold going on out there. I mean, seriously. Santa doesn't get overtime for this festive Easter gig. The bunny is essential, not the slightly rotund fellow in the red jacket and pants.

Maybe he can bring me some spoons.

# CHAPTER 22

## POLICE PRESENCE...

G'day, eh? A chilly, wintery, blustery day..and I have been blamed throughout the whole of it for the ensuing customary mid-April shaking of the heads in heaven without the use of Head & Shoulders.

A wee bit more in today's tidy tome pertaining to those officers of the law. A presence felt yet again today in our small community by the bay. Apparently, nothing we are to be concern with...which makes you even more concerned...just sayin. Can't they come up with another way to put it? "Nothing to see over here". "Pay no attention to that guy dressed in black with the weapons and mirror glasses" or, my personal favourite, "Stay The 'F at Home" you know, like that song everybody's playing all over right now. Pluto would call it worry balls for your worry wall.

So my worry balls are about done in. How to cook turkey leftovers the 37th different way; what to call the dog; what makes the propane stove sound like lift off at Cape Canaveral; how did I end up with no spoons even when the sleigh sat in the driveway, looking like it was delivering goodies, with snow and everything.....that deep rumble is the exhaust system chortling. That'll teach you to think about putting your top down in -6 weather. Like the guy who was actually swimming in the Bay the other day, while his bundled up wife held a towel. Nuts!

I think, no, I *know* I should probably talk to a shrink. Can you just hear it:

(Sotto voice) Hello, how may I help you?

(Me, hysterical) This is the 7th day of quarantine and my dish must've run away with the spoons....hello? Hello? Damn internet, calls are dropping all over the place.

I decide I'd better forgo spoon search for sock search. I'm tired of being cold, anybody else? Mid-April, this nonsense should be easing toward nicer days and warmer nights. I've been wearing the same double-thick, padded warm, cozy socks for three days. I think my feet stink worse than dog farts. They were my mom's, I think..the socks, not the feet, and she liked warm ones. I've washed them...a few times....but I think they're the warmest ones I have. I'd better change them. I need to find my big, thick "Canadian Olympic" fuzzy grey ones with the cute, little elf-like fringe around the top. I don't care what they look like, whose gonna see me???? I don't think the dog cares.. he's just jealous. He has white socks on each paw and can't ever change his. At least I get to do that, if I can find them. There they are, on top of the piano. Hey, if I had a dresser in my living room, they'd be in it! From the piano they go on top of the stove, once it gets back from outer space. Maybe it took the creature of the upper region with it when it blasted off. Haven't heard anything today but the pest guys were here this morning and they can't figure it out either. Well, if they can't figure it out, I don't know who is supposed to. Another vent, another venue for their one-act show.

The socks are warm now, maybe I can find an insulated coverall for indoor wear...maybe it'll look like a bulky track suit you wear inside. Maybe a velour coverall, that's back in, right? ....shiny zipper, smooth shiny material with two little pockets I can put crap in that I'll never find again. Like spoons. Velour always came in shiny colours too...Maroon, rust, my personal favourite, purple. We always got them for Christmas..mom, my sister and myself. Either Dad was bored with shopping or he thought we really wanted those. I don't know, you can't wear them out when you get one a year for 15 years. Maybe I could find them and make socks out of them....they might be here somewhere....

# CHAPTER 23

## CARDBOARD...

Hey there...set a spell. Take yer shoes off....just make sure you leave them at the door. Wash your hands. Ole Jed never seemed to be too worried about that, I don't think.

Today's mini missive brings greetings from the cardboard boxes alive and well and living in my kitchen, bedroom and front porch. These have taken on a new life as possible chew toys in addition to their current employment as containment containers of everything but loaf pans. I wonder, if I lay them off, can they apply for assistance? They could get recalled for other work, maybe for Amazon. They could explore strange new worlds, seek out new lives and new civilizations..boldly go....nowhere. No freakin' where. Not on a train, plane or automobile. Isolated corrugated city. If I liberated them, though, I'd have to find the shelves.....which are somewhere..out there. I don't know where the boxes could get enough masks and gloves to fit them if they made an essential trip.

But then, another cardboard box arrived today from the UPS guy. Oh bliss. But this one was good. You should've seen the look on the dog's face when he sniffed this big box that arrived. Did he bark, howl or even whine at the guy? No. Nothing. Watchdog protector fail. Not even, "hey dude, what're you up to over there with that box?" Nope. More like, "Oh. There's another box. Hey buddy, I'm new and even I can't wait to see where she's gonna put it. Get a load a' this!" But then he sniffed. The biggest, hugest sniff there ever was. Canine Nirvana. Wait just a minute. That's my box. That smells like my stuff.

A month's worth of dog food...ha. That'll teach him to have 'tude. "Wait.... lady...where you going with that? Come back, Auntie M....that's mine!" I

I wiped it all down after leaving it outside for a few hours and put it in the bunkie. Out of sight, since I don't have a shelf to put it on. Aroooooooooooooo!

We are also doing our homeschooling so this afternoon after Math (if you have one cookie, you don't automatically get two more) and English (trying out new names..No, Down and I Mean It!) it was time for music class. John Denver might be his favourite artist. I think he thought the bars were open again with all the dancing around going on. Then singing along with the band. Hound Dog Hop and Woo Woo Womble took place, followed by a lovely rendition of Get Down, You're Rockin The Trash Can. Only one encore and the tip jar was empty. I think more rehearsals are in order.

So 007.....since he seems to be shaken, not stirred and seems to have the ability to dance his way out of situations and ahem...got the girl...I think we should call him Bond.

# CHAPTER 24

## BONDING...

So Bond...is bonding. With the grass, with the trees, with the cardboard.... and with the neighbourhood. This morning, he lived up to his name and "bonded" with the creatures of the Bay. On his newly established tie line...I think he's playing baseball...maybe he's Barry Bonds...Maybe he's a singer... Gary "US" Bonds..or maybe he's just a bonded fool....He decided that one sniff out the back and it was time to break the ties that bound and head off to the neighbours to see what the what in their yard. There I am, 7:30 am, running after him up the road yelling, "Bond...Bond....No...stop..... down....sit......ah hell.....see ya later....." He went up the road and around the corner and stopped in the neighbouring yard, after knocking over a trash can and treeing a squirrel. Why the hell can't he tree the one in the attic??? Was he just practicing, a trial run, before the real thing?? The real thing is COKE and I don't think he's ever had any so why does he think a practice is ok. Maybe he would like some coke...some of you think I already have some....

I managed to grab him on the second pass, fumbling in the outfield in my infield garb, while holding onto the tie that refused to bind, out in my overnight bloomers. it's damn cold here, too. We were running through the snow, I might add....WITHOUT coffee....just add that to your mental tabulations. The dog was toast. When I finally grabbed the rope, he got pulled and yanked (maybe I should've called him Yank) back to the house and in the door...I don't CARE if you want to play in the yard. You broke the Play rope, bud. Ain't happening. So inside to watch me catch my breath, pour that ever-necessary first cup and sit down after my morning run. Over there...away from me right now..Mama not happy. I'm old...I don't do that nonsense anymore...getting older by the sprint.

He lay down, just like nothing ever happened. What a dog.

So now, we need a new tie-em up rope that won't break. The clasp broke, the rope is fine but I don't have the technology to attach a new one. I was able, after much searching, find another with better clasps and the battle was won. My god, I forgot how strong they can be. James had me shaken, stirred up and definitely shook in the shakey shakey maker. Coffee might not be enough for these shenanigans.

And Then...."gasp" once recovery, yogurt and a steady heart rate had been consumed and resumed, I went foraging in the beyond, while himself had a wee nap and enjoyed the nature. Lots of sniff but no snafu. Can I get an amen?

And you will NEVER guess what I found in my forage......

No...not Sam Elliott....sigh. Blessed are the non-believers. LOAF PANS. Seriously, I couldn't believe it either. The dish is still on a three-day pass with the spoons...dirty bugger. I'm still telling the electric frying pan to zap all of them when they come back. They're probably up in separate trees with the squirrel and Paul Newman having distant cocktails and laughing so hard.......

# CHAPTER 25

## FEELING OLD...

Good Sunday morning to you. Hope all are well and feeling fine. Random thoughts in the key of "Y".

Had an OMG moment today. Just the next one in a series of them lately, but hey. My oldest turned 36. I can't be that old. I actually have other kids that are my age but that's a whole other story best told at happy hour. Seriously. After the run for the squirrel dog the other day, I feel like I could be that old. I didn't know I could do that, hampered by pjs, but it's a new world out there. I don't think the neighbours have recovered. So the kid is 36. I have a velour tracksuit older than that. Even the new not-so-secret agent dog is 42 in people years. So the kid is still young but oh so wise! At least, that's what she tells me.

So here I am, feeling old, chilly at every venture out the door, creaking and groaning like WD40 has never been invented every time I try to turn around. The Peggy Lee song "Is That All There Is" comes into my foggy brain. Really. I sometimes wonder as I wander. Another old song - look it up. As I'm do do do lookin out the back door to the shed, I wonder where have all the flowers gone and when in the frozen frig are they coming back? The shed chortles with wicked abandon . Here you come again. But you can't always get what you want, you know. All I want are spoons. No no no no I can't take any more. In my midnight confession, she wore blue velour...the Polish Prince would be appalled.

An-y-way, I decided that between rounds of hunt and hound and sounding like I either need more vodka or much less, I would share some random acts of kindness that have come my way. A friend dropped off some excellent homemade soup and dog biscuits the other day for his royal houndness, which he loved. Another friend dropped burritos and brownies to the porch rail. Yummy! Thank you so much for all the thoughtful goodies and kind stuff. Makes it all a bit better ♥.

Just in case you were wondering, the old shed did cough up another little few pieces of the lost pie. The crockpot! Woohoo. Now I can crock all those random bits of frozen meat, just like me, into some sort of cornucopia of gastric delight. Maybe a roast with vegetables. Maybe chicken and spuds. Maybe some of the wine from the local store to go with it all. Oh joy and rapture unforeseen. The Sunday golf bag. You know, the little one that only holds half your clubs but makes you feel like a pro because they only seem to need half of their clubs. I never have the right half. At least now, I have a bag for them, having left mine in my other home so I had room for toilet paper and the aforementioned vodka. Mixing bowls, plastic containers and cookie sheets. I'm sensing a theme here. I almost feel normal. Put dinner in the crockpot, go golfing, come back and make Olive Garden cheese and garlic biscuits to go with it. Sounds too good to be true. I'll never be normal....

# CHAPTER 26

## NO PEE FOR YOU...

Hey everyone! Hope you're keeping well and keeping home. Sometimes you need to educate some folks. Like our Agent buddy Bond, here. Home is home. It's where the heart is, where they have to let you in if you go back there and where you're supposed to go pee in the yard first thing every morning.

I don't understand a dog that doesn't do that. I must be new. I didn't get the memo. Something. I thought it was common knowledge in the Book of Dogs, Chapter 1B, that after you wake up your human with nudges, hand kisses and gentle prodding with your head, that you sweetly, obediently go to the door while patiently waiting for your rope to be hooked up. Then you bound outdoors with the greatest of relief so you can make deposits in several locations prior to coming back in for breakfast. Somebody's dog was not copied on the memo.

After much cajoling, marching around the yard and saying "Bond..this time I mean it" you finally go back in and unhook it all. Did he sneak one in? Back inside we go and await the inevitable mishap on the carpet. Which doesn't happen. I thought all dogs were programmed the same. I'm almost afraid to look everywhere else inside. He wasn't out of my sight. Where could he have gone?

Meanwhile, back at the back door, our intrepid non-urinating carnivorous canine is all smiles and giggles, just eyeing the next opportunity to thwart the threat of tinkle. Jumping up and down...who can do that when you have to pee? Only somebody that does not have to. So, we have breakfast, coffee, read the paper, check the latest updates on every channel that ends in "news" and see what Pluto has to say today about the two legged crisis. After all of this, it is decidedly time to sally forth. Load me up, hook em on and let's go. First, it's chilly and squirrels are Everywhere. Just like CityTV used to be, thumbs up Mark Dailey. We stop, we point, we aim...aannd we keep walking. The geese on the bay are especially intriguing. Tail straight back and stock still. I think if I dropped the leash, he'd be across the park and in the water. Still no flush action. We continue up the road, with a little attitude, wanting to backtrack the shore. Nope. Don't need wet dog on top of full dog. We sidle along the edge of the road, sidle...almost like slinking only not quite as furtive. Sniffing here, sniffing there, trotting a tricky triad of stop, sniff, squat without squirt. I honestly am dumbfounded. My dog, the walking water tank. Just as suddenly, the sniffing ends and the squatting begins. Hallelujah! Once the cataract ceases, on we walk, a definite extra spring in the step now.

I don't understand the new guy. Who does that? Is he afraid of the avalanche? Terrified of the trickle? I wonder if it's just some weird form of morning jitters. Maybe some dogs are used to hours of that and his timer hadn't gone off yet. I hope he can relax a bit more and feel more comfortable. I certainly don't want him to feel like he's got to wait til noon if he's up late, I would feel like a bad dog mom. Agent 007, everywhere.....

# CHAPTER 27

## MOVE YOUR STUFF...

Goooood Morning! Wake up, sit up and let's get going.

Foraging. Back to hunting and seeking. Today, I seek to find....my sanity which I've left behind.. hee hee, not really..hey, I heard that....

How is everyone holding up out there? At least you have spoons. Today's wish of wonderment is wondering how to get the tv cabinet into the living room from the kitchen. The movers put I there. I don't see them coming back, somehow. It is huuuuuge...large and unwieldy so I'm not sure I can do it myself. I'd love to set the rest of my kitchen up, you know, display all the fun things I've found, use them, even. Some placemats, plates, ahem..cutlery.. eat soup....just sayin. I would love to sit in there beside the fire and have my tea. So far, I've got the sea of cardboard moved out of the way. I did the "eye" measure. The cabinet will fit through the living room door, let's hope so, since it was in there before. The piano is in the way. Hmm. It is up on specially made wheel blocks, for hardwood floors, all lovely padding underneath and everything. Well, in this house where the only place that doesn't have carpet is the bathroom, I'm thinking these delightful holder/uppers are doing a fine job holding up the whole process. If the thing didn't weigh so much, I could slide it off them and wheel it where I want it. Since it does, I can't. I also can't slither the cabinet past it as there isn't any slither room. None. Hey dog, you're not helping. Can't you "Bond" this and make it so? Oh, wrong movie. Do I want to watch tv in the kitchen? I could, I suppose. How many splitters and channel changers am I going to need for that? I can't even find the converter I'm supposed to have for the tv now. Maybe, just maybe, I think with intensity, I could use the cupboard for dishes and a pantry. I propose a Repurpose. All my cookery goods in one place. A special shelf just for oatmeal. Dijon oatmeal..hey, if it works for Steven Page....Flour - I have kinds already. White and metal. Packaged and tinned. Woohoo, rolling now. Salt, pepper and garlic salt. But not just any garlic salt, the kind with little flakes of onion tucked away in there. Yum. Right in that cute little spot where you'd keep your old VHS tapes. Perfect. Ok, now the sugar, the baking soda, then that cake mix that will expire in 4/04/20. Might have to make that tomorrow. Look at me, Space saving already. Oh look...room for a loaf pan 😊. I look around, seeing possibilities everywhere I turn. The pasta packages, right there in the old alcove for the outlets. I can haul the old fake wood back off the thing, nobody needs an oval tv-shaped hole on the back of their shelf. Crap will fall through, though. Much like this paragraph. A spot for the fancy little crackers I could have with my tea. Just slide the tv shelf out, just like a real pantry, and I wouldn't have to dig for anything. Just the aforementioned sanity. I think it's hiding under the piano.

# CHAPTER 28

## UNBONDED...

Good morning everyone! Hope it's a good one so far. Coffee up!

So, our intrepid, devil-may-care new guy pooch has been having a bit of a rough time adjusting to his new surroundings. He seems to be having a hard time understanding, "No, that's a window, we don't go through those" and/or "Nope, down, we don't ram the door either or we'll break it." Early in the adventure, he was pushing and shoving all the time. I thought it was just part of the learning curve. It seems I might've been incorrect..mistaken... even the "w" word - wrong. Our poor fella is still having a hard time being inside. He is pretty good outside, for a little bit, then decides he should be chasing/running after anything. I think he gets bored with the routine, not ever having had one. When you're used to following your every sniff to see where it takes you, you can see where he might be struggling with the whole rope/tied/not free part of living in a human community. He's also a hunting dog and the other day, when he took off after the squirrel, was his natural thing. I, sadly, don't have lots of room for him to roam and run.

I talked with the shelter to see if they had any insight and they said they had been concerned about this very thing, when a hunting dog of his age goes to a home to live. It was decided, with a very heavy heart, to try to find him a farm or somewhere with lots of land for him to roam. I am very upset, however, he's not happy. It's so sad because he's a very sweet boy. I'm going to miss you, Bond ♥. I hope you get a forever home to run and hunt.

# CHAPTER 28B

Hey y'all. The deed is done but one final footnote to our tale of Bond. As I was taking him out after one last tour before getting in the car, he looked at the car and said No Freakin Way and slipped his collar. He took off at breakneck speed about half mile down the road to the bush, along the lake. I'm running along calling him, not seeing him. I catch sight of him down there and I run back around the house and grab the car. I figure if I try and run, he'll be gone before I can get there. I take off in the car and get there, getting out slowly so I don't spook him. He's just standing there looking at me like "What...?? You lookin for me??" Jesus H Christ on a cracker. Huff and puff. I managed to grab his collar and wrestle him into the car, where he proceeded to lay down ever so nicely. Eye roll.

I got him the rest of the way without further incident but as a parting shot, I think it was a doozy. Have fun on the farm, 007, miss ya.

# CHAPTER 29

Meh.....

Hey everybody! Hope you're bright eyed etc., etc. Feels like a Pinky & The Brain moment...same thing every day. Or Groundhog Day....again. Anybody else getting tired of same old same old? My heart aches for Nova Scotia and all affected. Coffee's perking, hang in.

I decided I'd have a baloney sandwich and ice cream for breakfast. Not nutritional at all, but damn, it felt good. I'm getting tired of cooking for me, too. Anybody else? I know about four go-to things then I have to get creative. The extra Q calories are going to be very telling in about three weeks. Lunch: cheese and crackers, that wasn't too bad. Dinner: Time to straighten up. I check out the freezer...meh. I look in the pantry...everything needs a spoon. I check the other fridge. Aha! Healthy Choice rice bowl and chicken. Perfect. Don't look at the calories or sugar content, just eat it and be glad it's not Kawartha Dairy Salty Carmel Truffle. Sometimes, a girl has to to change up her oatmeal. On top of the five coffees already to keep warm, plus the one on the way back from town. Then, to the cardboard cleanup. If you joined me yesterday, there was a heap of cardboard on the back porch that got "relocated" with some help. There's a burn ban on everywhere here so it will have to wait for recycling pick up.

I was trying to figure out if I could use some of it for something else. Besides just a cardboard box. I mean, I could make a craft. I could, if I were (was?) crafty. I will also get enterprising and use some to try and move the piano and the TV cabinet. Then I thought of a makeshift closet organizer. That has definite possibles. Makeshift, because I think I my closet shelves are MIA with the spoons and I don't know where they went. Or even if they want to come home. I know, I know, ask the car. It just rolls it's headlights and rolls up the windows. It ain't easy, being me. They aren't in the shed, believe it or not. There's just more cardboard in there. Maybe I could stack the boxes like little shelf units in my empty closet room. I could unpack the rest of the suitcases and put the stuff away. Yeah! That would work, until I find my shelves. I like it. So I take the eight boxes I have and start to see how they can stack together. Right off, size matters. You know it does, I can hear you from here. Big on the bottom then smaller above that then smaller... It's boxes. Most things go from bigger to smaller. A natural order. But I digress. Stacking boxes. So when you unwrap the package...what?? Sometimes they have an outer wrap. The outer wrap then the seams. They have to be even or the wrap doesn't come off right. So you get them lined up then you pull the wrap off ever so slowly, peeling it back. You can't rush it or it will rip. I think. It's been so long since I peeled a wrap, I'm not even sure I remember how.

Once you get it unwrapped, then you need to put them one after the other, or even side by side, so that when its done, you have a nice stack, ready to tuck away back in the closet. For your stuff. Maybe I could use the rest to make an upright dresser.....

# CHAPTER 30

Maybe......

Morning! Coffee, yogurt & oatmeal. Gather around.

It was noted yesterday by my esteemed cuz B, that my sanity could definitely be in question. True dat! I think everyone's is, right now. Sometimes, as I'm spinning out on that carousel of life, I think I want off. Done, kaput, had it. It's not about missing spoons, it's about missing everything. Spoons are the least of my problems. A half-empty house, a porch full of strewn cardboard, all pale with our world at large. Perspective is everything. That being said, onto today's mishaps of misfortune.

The pest remover dudes were back today. Hallelujah! We think he/it/them are gone. Paul Newman has left the building. Probably off to his latest meet up with Joanne Woodward- the lucky blue-eyed bugger! At least he got to go somewhere. Maybe he needed groceries- they were worried he'd want mine but thankfully that didn't happen. He was wearing his face mask so he could go shopping if he wanted. As for tea and toast, he never showed up for that either. I can be thankful he was evicted with no forwarding address. So they closed up the hole and said so long! I forgot to ask if there's a warranty and a No-Return policy.

I also decided today to cook. Sakes alive! A new leaf...no more breakfast bologna. Back to yogurt & oatmeal for me. I'll find all the weight I lost if I keep that up. Although they did say if you're eating comfort food, carry on and worry about it later. Ya, worry later when I'd have to do the same darn thing all over again. It would be a whole lot bigger worry, then, too. Who am I kidding? I'm gaining on it now. I could walk more but I really need to find my bike. That would be great. I could ride hither and yon. I usually know whether hither is but yon is a bit elusive. I think the bike is in the shed.......

Oh my god. It is.....but it's in the little shed. Phew. Two sheds and a bunkie. That small one only giggles. It doesn't outright laugh and guffaw. Just a snort, a mild chuckle. So I go foraging..again...I haven't been in this little lean-to since this time last year....oh my what secrets does it hold? I won't be finding out any time soon because I can't find the key. I look up and down, here and there, even in the elusive yon....nothing. None of the keys fit that lock. Whahhhhhh! All I want to do is get my bike. Maybe there's a few spoons hiding behind the shovels and rakes, who knows!?! Maybe I .....maybe nothing. Nothing left to maybe. Maybe I need to get the bolt cutters. Get me a new lock. Yup. That's what I'll do. Okay, bolt cutters. Come out, come out wherever you are...Big Shed? Nope. Bunkie? Nope...running out of viable options here...Back room? Nope. Guess we know where this is going. Jesus. Somebody just smack me now.

Seriously.

# CHAPTER 31

We Rise Again, to Nova Scotia.

Good morning my fellow isolated souls! How is everybody doing today? Hopefully, coffee or the morning bevvy of your choice is warming your tattered heart and giving breath to your every whim and wonder.

I'm wondering about this whole freezing thing coming to the end of April. To my southern friends, it doesn't apply. You folks are floating in your own beer, already. To the rest of us, Ugh. So the ugh has kept me inside, chillin in more ways than one, and hoping for reprieve.

For one thing, adventures to sheds of all sizes is temporarily on hold as my fingers thaw out from constant cold metal and warm phone. The contrast is frightening! I am also waiting before I chat with the car about all the missing items around here. I don't think they're in there, however, somebody is withholding evidence.

The lock/key thing..well, I have a team of forensic missing stuff people looking into it. They'll contact my people when their people know something. I'm thinking that since that shrimpy shed is also withholding evidence, the forensics should be using a fine toothed comb in their investigation. The secrets are many, info is few.

Many thanks for all the super ideas. I even tried some of them. The bolt cutters, gun, bomb and crowbar are all MIA. They are snickering with every other missing thing and will, one day, return with some kind of bang. The You Tube video was quite detailed and informative on how to pick locks. I had no idea there was so much info out there. The metal pin insert in the key hole looked easy enough. Tried that, didn't make any headway. I couldn't get any purchase on the tumbler. That's lock-speak for it didn't work. I couldn't rub the side of the lock to free up the pins either, as it's solid metal. The tool for that job will be re-acquired after the B&E.

I'm also thinking that in the midst of all this, since I can't quite perform this B&E as everything I'd need is already a hostage in there, I might as well try another project. I can hear you from here....But this one is safe. What could happen? I could use an office. With what shall I office, I office, I office, with what shall I office, Dear Liza, with what? You know you sang it.

I have a table, a laptop, a phone. Cables, all the requisite holders, stands and paper. Even a printer and stand. So where, in this half empty sanctuary, shall I set that up? I have some space in the living room. Space in the closet room, since I have no shelves right now. There's always the attic room....uh no. Stairs..that's for kids and loud music. Not old mothers with rubber lined slippers and permanent frostbite. I'm thinking a tiny space in the living room would suffice. Not where the tv cabinet will go once the cardboard jungle is used as a slide, over closer to the sliding door buddy Bond decided he should vault through. I can see the sheds, yard and the bunkie. The sheds won't be able to plot the takeover of The Bay since I will have a eye on them all day. It will be perfect. What could go wrong?

What Went Wrong...or all the things that could go wrong, did, and then some.....

## CHAPTER 33

Hello, walls. Floors, ceilings, windows. Agh! It's another day, same as the other days. They all end in "Y". Coffee time, y'all. What happened on the weekend?

I got frickin' spoons! That's what happened! Yeehaw! And now, back to our regularly scheduled program.

I decided this morning that I should cook, since it was Sunday. I have been cooking but there's something about Sunday dinner that just makes you smile. I remember the ham and scalloped potatoes, the barbeque and potato salads, the roasts with mashed potatoes . . . a theme is becoming evident. We ate huge on Sundays and it seemed to include lots of potatoes. Leftovers were, and are, the bomb. Nothing better, to me, than the leftover vegetables the next day with either butter or gravy, all warmed up. That oatmeal is not going to cut it.

So, I got out a roast—not just any old roast, a beautiful, plentiful, bountiful roast for one. This cooking frenzy we're all on must continue! Thaw said roast, gather the veggies, crockpot at the ready, and we're off. In it goes, plus beef broth for liquid, onions, carrots, sweet potatoes, onion soup mix, salt, pepper, a hint of garlic. Eight hours later, voilà! Not vodka. I said voilà. As in, Great Scott, Captain, it's done! A good one it was, too. I made stew with the leftovers and more voilà; it'll be even better tomorrow. You didn't know you'd get dinner along with the movie.

Speaking of movies, screen time is up at least 50 percent with lots of FaceTime, Messenger and Houseparty get-togethers. Had gatherings online with family and friends today; good laughs and great to see faces!

After my cooking extravaganza in the kitchen with my crockpot and spoons, I was feeling pretty good about Sunday. I thought I would get outside and do things with my newly liberated lawn and garden tools. I didn't need the red wok for anything but it's ok, it can wait until I find the cord . . .

I got the stuff out and it started to rain. And get chilly. It was supposed to be warm and fuzzy today. The weather gods lied, although I imagine they have a bit more on their plate just now besides no rain so I can rake. The cardboard sea is ready for recycling.

Snow White and the Seven Guys you don't mention on television were watching in awe. I think Grumpy was eying up Doc, trying to pick a fight. Dopey had used up his allotted four plants and was looking to zip one of Happy's when he wasn't looking. He figures Happy is happy enough. Sleepy and Bashful were playing Go Fish until Sneezy let one go and blew the cards all over the yard. They are bored too, staring at each other all winter without moving, and now that spring is here, they were hoping for a little more action. You know, cocktails and dancing down at the bar, maybe see what Sleeping Beauty, Cinderella, and Rapunzel were up to. But Sleeping Beauty was having another nap, Cinderella wasn't done making Sunday dinner, and Rapunzel was cutting her own hair. She'll be busy with that 'til everyone else gets liberated.

# CHAPTER 34

Good Day. Snuggle up with your cup. An interesting day at The Bay. Or a bit of unease in the trees . . .

I've shared about the shifty shed, the crafty car, and the brazen bunkie; we now have the catacomb cellar. In the deep, dark denizens of below, live the sumptuous pump and its buddy, the powerful water whisker—whaddya want . . . it's early. This morning, laundry day, I went to wash my hands, yet again, when nothing happened. I mean, I tried to wash them but nothing came out of the tap. The laundry had worked but the water tap didn't. Sigh upon freakin' sigh. There is not enough coffee/vodka/beverage-of-your-choice for this. Today or any day. Putting down my hand soap, I head for the kitchen to try that tap. Nothing. Check the breaker panel, all good. So what the . . . wait. The electrical hookup. I go to the back room (all nefarious deeds of the world happen in a back room) and lo and behold—low, because it is down low—the electricity wasn't electric-ing. There was no jive on the juice. I tried the power bar connecting the whole schmozzel and there arose such a clatter that I figured all was well. Nope. Soon as my hand came off, so did the power. Again. The same. Okeydoke. A power bar was required. I hunt up and down, in and out, and find the one I was going to use for the office set up. Oh, the supreme sacrifices one must make. So, I switch all the stuff around and eureka! Look at me, all techy tech. There was power. All the things started running and making noise. Phew.

I carry on. You know there's more because I'm only part way down the page and there's never just one thing that happens. You aren't that new and even I'm reluctant to believe I can get away with one mishap per twenty-four-hour time slot. So, as I was saying before I so rudely interrupted myself, I've now headed outdoors to rake and tidy, do all those outside things you can't do inside. I'm busy doing the things when my ever-present phone goes off with a text. *Come on out and say hi.* I go around, it's buddy Bob from the Rail on his way home to Lindsay from an errand. Woohoo! We have a delightful socially distant visit, complete with far away beverages, then he heads home. So great to see him! I carry on, by this time heading back in to see to some dinner. I go into the back room to grab a few things from fridge #2 and as I'm turning around, I notice the sun shining quite brightly on the walls. At least, it would be if the room faced the west . . . starboard might be shining green but port is definitely glowing red. I look wildly for ships. Only, it's a red light on the wall. The holding tank alarm 🔔. And it's full. No flush, no laundry, no copious washing of hands. For those of you who were ever in doubt, yes, I guess I am totally full of $@&#.

Stay tuned tomorrow for "As the plot thickens and gets stuck" or "Please Release Me."

Wash your hands, if you can . . .

# CHAPTER 35

Good Morning All & Sundry.

Well, for those faithful followers, yesterday was, indeed, my birthday. I turned sixty years young, although some days it feels like 120. Thank you for all the good wishes. I decided, since it was my QBD (Quarantine BDay) and I was self-isolated like everyone, that I would forego the big party, the call from the Queen, etc., but I'd be darned if it was going by without something. My wonderful camp girls had planned an online party for this evening and my special tribe of happy hour girls this afternoon so I wanted something to share virtually. Of course, since you can't really share right now, that means it's all for me anyway, but I like to make it look like I'm thinking of everyone. So, I decide I'm baking cupcakes. Here's yours, here's yours . . . I figure I'll get to eat at least seven of them, you know, to be hospitable. So, I look to see what I have and land sakes, I have an imported red velvet cupcake mix . . . just what the birthday doc ordered. I excitedly begin gathering the essentials. Egg—check. Oil—I'm sure some kitchen STP is in there. Check. Water— check. Ok! I've got it—oh wait. Cupcake pans. I go to the cupcake pan place and reach in and find cookie sheets, cake pans, even the Bundt pan

. . . but no huffin' puffin' muffin tins. Seriously. Of course, it's never easy here. Eye roll optional. They are cavorting with the damn spoons in the Mediterranean making mini muffin cups and demitasse spoons. What else can I use? I check the box. Eight-by-eight cake pan. Perfect. I get that ready and then reach for the mixer. Nothing electric here. This one takes two hands to operate since it came over to the New World with the toaster. I start spinning that baby like a 1965 roundabout carousel. Surprised some of us are still alive. Soon, the oven is ready but I'm starting to smell some fragrances that don't belong. I'm also seeing smoke coming out of the vent. I open the oven and discover smoke everywhere completely obliterating the inside. I guess the lasagna the other day must've dripped more than I thought. I maneuver the racks so I can wipe the bottom with a wet rag. Nope. Seems to be adding to the smoke situation, not to mention avoiding the ouch factor. Not the most auspicious approach. I decide the toaster oven is the answer. Get that going while the oven cools down. I guess self-cleaning really is an essential service in an oven. Pressing that button, even more of a public service.

So, as I'm getting this all going, I decide I need birthday appetizers. Chips & dip will do it. Not fancy but hey, wait for Release Day for caviar, devilled eggs, and potato skins. Add a Georgian Bay Vodka Smash and Bob's your uncle. He actually was, you know. Yours too? We can share.

Between the online keg parties, I got a message from my neighbour to come outside. When I got out there, my next-door family and their up-the-street family bubble sang a socially distant Happy Birthday then tossed over a bag of banana muffin and peanut butter cookies (at least somebody has muffin tins around here) and a bag with the biggest, heaviest, warmest socks I've ever seen! Oh my goodness . . . a coven of coziness and caring.

I'm happy to report that my happy hours were happy, my cake delightfully non-shared with others, and my chips and dip all gone. Hold up two hands and wave them when you say that.

For your next birthday, I recommend you keep calm and eat cake and drink vodka with your socks on. Helluva plan! Thank you to everyone who made turning sixty just a little bit more ♥.

# CHAPTER 36

Well, hello out there. Coming to you live and in virtual colour from my chair with my coffee.

Grab yours and pitter patter.

I decided since I'm oh so much older now, not necessarily wiser, it was time to take stock. Not that there's much in here to take stock of. My kitchenware is forming its own society in another land and my house is somewhat shambling around me. It's time, I say to myself, with authority, to refresh and freshen up. I, fortunately, was able to do that rather nicely since the waste retrieval management company read: honey wagon did their thing with the whatsit tanks. Summer rates—woohoo! I then began to look around the place.

Some things need a brush up, you know, for when the rest of my belongings come home to roost, or fester, as the case may be. I look, up, waaaay up—tell me you're not looking for the Giant in the room—and I see some ceilings that could use some touching up. Well, says I, I think I can do that without too much trouble. What could happen?? I hear you all, I'm not deaf, just more senior, k? I have painted before and even since I've lived here so it's not new. Mind you, painting neurasthenia (you know the drill . . . look it up) has been known to strike the unwary at the most inopportune times. This, I think, is something I can do fairly easily.

I get out the trusty laptop, which we are all doing lately, and get onto my local "buy everything in Canada, especially those tires" site and I find what I'm looking for fairly easily . . . ceiling paint, how difficult can it be to find? Not like it's Cerulean Blue by Benjamin Moore.

I choose my brand, specifically made to cover up a multitude of ceiling sins in one easy roll, and proceed to checkout, adding said roller along the way. I've got the rest of the accoutrements assembled. I get to the "put your Code in here for extra points" part and it all goes for a flying leap. I put the code in . . . won't accept the password. Ok, let's set a new one, then. So, I go through all the steps to make that happen and we come to "send a verification code" so I wait patiently because I know things are busy. I finally get the code, it won't accept the code. I try again. I get a new code. It then tells me my password doesn't match theirs. I think, alrighty, maybe I need to reset the password. I reset the password, that works, then I get a new code and the password won't work. So now I'm getting angry. Not Donald Dick angry "Oh boy, oh boy, oh boy" but full out Yosemite Sam . . . "Oooooooooh." Then annihilation.

I step back, take a breath. It's not their fault, I reason. It's not mine. I certainly have done everything they asked. Could I have found another way to do it? No. There's only one way to do this. Finally, I come up with a password, enter it in and get the "we will send you a verification" note. Again. I got this far, again . . . a tentative fist awaits raising. Well, I do verify that I have done this all correctly. In between entering the password, right before I start to enter the new code, I receive a pop up that says "How would like to take our survey? How was our service today?". . . Now I need a new laptop . . .

# CHAPTER 37

Today, we are discussing furniture. Not the "oh, isn't that a cute little French provincial night table." I mean, big, hulking, take-no-prisoners-type monsters. The "I love you but I'll leave you right frickin' here if you give me any more problems" type. I decided I'd better try to reposition the piano and the tv cabinet so I could re-locate my kitchen, currently enjoying a cabinet and a second cardboard sea. I have done this kind of thing before. Even though I'm, ahem, advancing in years, I still think I've got it. I found out today I left it somewhere in my forties and I would like it back, thank you very much. I'm very used to doing my own stuff, sometimes with a bit of help. Normally, I'd find the kids (as they are younger and less breakable than me) and we'd make it happen. So, I begin with the nemesis, the piano. Their piano, I might add. I can't wait to hear the backlash. A retirement plan was me learning how to play it. If I ever retire, I'll get right on that. I know the cardboard under the feet trick for moving furniture—I get the cardboard. The piano already has feet, under the little teensy, weensy wheels your great-grandmother had on her spinet. Flat feet, so no dancing or long walks for this baby. Specially made for hardwood floors with lovely felt bottoms and everything. Not for thick pile berber carpet. I huff and I puff; you would've thought I was finally making muffins. I finally huff and puff the back off the foot on the front side. Then the front off the foot on the back side, then the piano hits the floor. Sounds like a flat version of *Bumble Bee*. Or *The Entertainer*. Since I lost Paul Newman, maybe I can have Robert Redford. It's starting to feel like a sting. Copious huffing now. Now other two sides— keep up, there are four—and we have an even flatter bee . . . B? Then the moving and grooving across the carpet, could've been a sock hop, except nobody was wearing socks. Well, I was wearing huge cozy ones but not without heavy duty shoes for this dance hall duet. I finally heave and ho and shove the 750-pound marvel into the wall, nearly ending up back in the kitchen without using the door. Sit down, tea and rest, and Awaaaaaay We Go! This time, it's the cabinet's turn. Again, with the cardboard. This chartreuse is worthy of Fred and Ginger. I have to get it the ten feet to the living room door then through the door then across the twenty-foot room. Right there, I've got more feet than inches. Slither and slide, push and pull, propel and impel, it's all going on. Put another dime in the record machine. It's Moonwalk time! I heard the car sniggering through the window. Almost an hour later, the dancing was done, the band quit, and the server had crashed behind the bar. Now, the pieces are in place, the place is in pieces, and my back could've done its last shuffle off to Buffalo except the border is closed. Besides, where was Irv Weinstein last time I needed him—off looking for missing children.

So now, I have two more big pieces in place. I sit down, have another tea, and I put some heat on my back, in the form of an expired (2014) heat pocket in an old sock and sit back and look at my handiwork. I'm feeling pretty good about it, too, until I look over at the tv. Now, I'm afraid to move it into the cabinet. It'll take somebody under thirty-five to hook it all back up again.

# CHAPTER 38

It's always a beautiful day in the neighborhood when your local agency store calls to tell you your favourite Kim Crawford wine is in and it's ready for pick up. Woohoo . . . so sneakily sneaky and oh, so divine! Makes me feel like I have to go there and say a password through the sliding window. I want to tell them "Boris sent me" and see what happens. I might end up with a dry weekend.

Among other things on the list today is, hopefully, picking up paint. And hanging racks and ever-infernal muffin pans. I swear, the world is out to get me. If they really are, are you really paranoid? Inquiring minds and all that. Since it's become a sunny day, it's time to get some outside work done. I see the car edging over to see what Snow and the Dudes are up to. If they can whisper, so can I. Hah. Now the neighbours are staring, wondering if I've dropped my phone since I'm whispering at ground level. I don't want them to see or hear me. Snow & the Heavy 7. I mean, they'll tell the car. If they hear me, I'll just have to figure out Plan B. According to a good friend, everyone needs one.

Today's Plan B consists of not picking up paint, racks, or tins. As noted, it's a lovely day, today. I hear Ella singing and there's no one there. Except a few guys suggesting I do some whistling while I work. Not sure why they care, they're just standing there, gawking at the girl. Not working.

I decide it's time to sweep some more large back deck. Got to move the back deck furniture on and get the *gasp* cushy cushions. If it's gonna be nice out, you want to be ready. It might only last about six and half minutes but I'll be ready. I might even downgrade the parka for an anorak. Hey guys, ya wanna give me a hand? Stop that blasted whistling and grab an end . . . not that end. Huh. Send a bunch of boys . . .

I get two of about eight pieces of outdoor rattan onto the deck. What's that I hear? The happy hour bell? Could it be? Yes, 4 pm, and it's time for the Hour of Power, Happy Hour, coming to you live from a social media device near you! Come one, come all. Forget your troubles, c'mon get happy, you better chase all your cares away! While you're busy shouting hallelujah, don't wave your arms around and spill your drink. The people get so upset when you do that. But there aren't any people. Whose gonna know? Sleepy, quit that snoring, they'll hear you.

# CHAPTER 39

Today's vintage vignette comes to you from the yard. It's coffee time at the lake this morning. Nothing better than a lovely hot cup a cuppa when your feet hit the floor. The only thing better is having some in stock when you reach for the pot.

I received a message this morning from #2 daughter & hubby asking if I might have any extra coffee in stock as their recent grocery shop failed to yield any on the shelves. No coffee?? Fightin' words if I ever heard 'em. I suggested they come out for a morning chalice of caffeine in the yard and we could sip in distant harmony. I could also share some beans with the weans. Look it up.

They must've been definitely in short supply; they were in the driveway and rushing to the cups and chairs I had set out before the pot had even perked a full pop.

We sat far apart and talked of close up things: work, life, music, friends, and I was so thankful they thought to come out and share a morning patter and a need indeed. A mom can still be a mom if you can help.

It was onto yard work after that, since I'd started in the yard, it seemed only right. The back deck was beckoning, again, the dudes and dudette just stared and stared. The rattan deck furniture was unearthed from the earth behind The Shed, and said Shed was laughing as usual. Too bad the furniture had to stay outside. It would've, apparently, been so much better in there. Now I'm laughing. Since it didn't do too good of a job on the furniture cushions, lost the spoons, and fessed up only one swoopy golf shoe, I figured no comment was comment enough. Don't poke the bear. Around the other side of the house, the whistling continued. I'm glad the breeze is picking up off the lake since it drowns out the sound.

I think I need virtual psychiatry. Happy hour at 4, bring your own vodka.

# CHAPTER 40

Forty days!!! Forty days—they say we'll be back home in forty days . . . well, at least the gypsy woman will be. As for the rest of us, we're already there and hoping the light at the end of the tunnel is not a train. I guess we'd better ask the Hawk; he seems to be the only one who knows.

First things first. Coffee. Then Paint pick-up!! Ya-freakin-hoo, got the message this morning at 7 am that it was ready—along with hanging bars and muffin pans and a roller . . . make that movie stop, I dare ya.

Pick up was slicker'n spit on a doorknob. Drive in, give your order number, Shazam, it's coming out and into the trunk of your car, no-contact delivery. If only the paint could get on the wall in the same fashion. Sometimes, in less pristine scenarios, I have too much contact with the paint, the roller, the wall, the floor, furniture and so forth. Good thing I have about five tarps all ready; I hope it's enough. A very socially distant drive-by coffee with friends, E & L, and it was home to unload the booty and begin getting organized. I hear all of you laughing, instead of just the shed.

I also took some time to put two of the clothes bars together, so there! Now installed with the requisite clothing and shoes. Yay—something normal! Who knew? Normal. Hah. I'm looking in the mirror seeing forty-five days since my last haircut and thinking if I could find the long-handled hedge trimmers, I could open a business in the backyard. Why not? I don't have a hedge. I've got a 70's shag going on, thinking I look like every girl in my 1976 yearbook. It must be all the rage. Everybody's got one.

Because racks and shelves and paint mean possible incoming clutter, I decided last night it was time to take the Clutterbug Quiz. This was sent to me by my good friend C, who is the Martha Stewart of shelving. It is now official that I am a Clutterbug "Bee" "who needs to learn to let go, who tends to keep things 'just in case' you may need it someday. If you don't love it and haven't used it in a year, get rid of it." I howled. My stuff has been spending a year getting rid of me. Not sure they have a category for that . . . Cricket, Bee, Butterfly, or Ladybug. I see a planet of household things in limbo . . . hopping, buzzing, floating, and crawling around, waiting to be reclaimed by their owner. The karma of this is getting to me.

So, as I figure out how to BEE organized, BEE ruthless in my purging, BEE the BEE who finally gets it all where it's going before I forget where it all is, I decide I'm just not rushing with this. It will get where it's going in its own good time. No rush, no foul. No mad panic to hunt and gather. I've got enough stuff for the next couple of pandemics so I've got lots of time to put it all away.

# CHAPTER 41

Oh my god, coffee & Baileys! Today, I'm thinking the place is haunted. Newman, are you back? Phone calls are dropping left and right, video calls are freezing and online meetings are disconnecting. Before, I would've said it is volume of traffic causing all these twenty-first century problems. Now, I'm not so sure. In my hallway I have several pictures of the house in various incarnations over the decades, after its origins as a sawmill. It was the local store and post office for many years after the sawmill closed and the land sub-divided. The small store building was later moved next door and now serves as a bunkie. One of the pictures on the wall is of the land around 1985 and it was this one that decided it was time to fly off the wall and crash on the floor. I was on the phone at the time, the call disconnecting and me yelling loudly during the ruckus. Amid glass shards and frame parts, I hopped and tiptoed through the wreckage and had a new look at the pictures as I picked it all up.

A sawmill, a store, post office, summer cottage, and now snowbird home for the not rich and certainly not famous me. Right about where Snow and the Seven Slackers are today was the area where you and I, in our six-year-old lives, would've had a Melorol ice cream and bag of penny candy. A quick skip down to the lake to play on the new swings and slide while the Royal Mail packet boats cruised by from one waterfront village to the next. Logs, like those that fill the lake bottom, were often milled here and deadheads are a common sight in spring as the lake is quite shallow, by most lake standards.

The land, sloping down from the high hill at the south, was the scene of much activity for a century and more. I'm wondering if they knew back then that this would one day be presided over by some concrete statues and a wishing well. I think somebody's ghost must've wanted to play with the dudes and maybe share an ice cream to go. They didn't have to hang up on me on almost every call and meeting and break a picture to get my attention. Maybe they are buddies with the shed.

# CHAPTER 42

## Happy Day After Cinco de Mayo!

Coffee time, for the "am" challenged. I hope you enjoyed the story on the origins of my house. I'll keep digging; hopefully I can scare up more history on the place.

Yesterday had its haunted happenings, today was no better. Every single call, video meeting, and even a phone call just next door was interrupted with dead air, a dead screen, or some combination of dead silence. The only positive part of it all was the shed was silent, too. Maybe Newman did chew some wires.

I was talking on various phone calls this morning and several people figured I'd hung up on them. One of the later calls was with Service Canada; good thing it didn't happen then. I couldn't believe, with all that is going on, that when they said they'd contact me within two business days with an access code, they actually did. Who knew a pandemic would be good for customer service? I figured they would be so swamped they might've gotten back to me by the time it's all over. I sat still, made sure I didn't move around, got an arm cramp so I didn't disturb the signal. It's all how you hold your tongue. I gave the woman a start, though.

"Are you applying for the CERB?" she asked me. (This is the Canadian Emergency Response Benefit.)

"No, I'm not."

"Pardon me?"

"No, I'm not."

"Did you say you weren't applying?"

"Yes, I did."

"May I ask why?"

"Because I don't qualify."

"How do you know you don't qualify? The questions on the application will determine if you qualify."

"I don't qualify because I don't work, didn't work, haven't worked, didn't quit work, and am not trying to work."

"Oh."

I wish trying to repatriate my stuff with my house qualified as a job, though; I'd be all over it. It's turning out to be a career. I don't think she's ever talked to somebody like me before. I'm given to understand not many have. One of my often-disconnected, seldom-misdirected, happy hour conferences today revealed a concern for people's mental health during these difficult times. People in general, me specifically. As I was laughing wildly and waving my drink, all while trying to string two words together without getting cut off, she might've had a point. "Who ya gonna call?"

# CHAPTER 43

Today's anecdotal affair is a recitation of several things. I was very thankful for all the positive feedback I received about the history of the house. I'm looking into more research on that to see what can be found. Stay tuned. Film won't be at 11 but maybe by 12 or 1. If the signal works. Muffins . . . finally, muffins.

So, I got the new muffin pans and made the muffins . . . epic fail. The ghosts were not unhappy that they didn't get any. I would like to say it was the pans . . . but, it wasn't. Maybe they need to be broken in? Maybe I'm the broken one. Quiet, if you can't say something nice . . . Burnt them, right to the bottom. They tasted ok, except for the blackened sole and crusty edges part. Sigh. I can't even make a muffin in a new pan. I was lamenting that today, while I was trying to get ready to paint. It is chilly in that porch. Although by Happy Hour at 4:30 or so, it was lovely. Nothing's easy. Drop the drop sheets, scrape the tape, and find the broom handle. Did you honestly expect it to go well? Those things in themselves are a recipe for disaster. Who doesn't know where their tape and broom handle are? Thank you to lovely neighbour "F" for porch dropping some of theirs. Not everything went wrong today, although calls and video messages were still dropping with disgusting regularity. It's nice to know some things remain the same. I did, however, have several important calls for which I ended up outside in my socks, on the walkway, standing slightly sideways on one foot so they didn't disconnect. I'm now starting to think this is normal behaviour. So are my neighbours. By the time all this was over, the front outside porch was lovely and warm in the sun and a glass of wine looking at the lake was just the recipe I needed.

Keep Calm and don't burn your muffins.

# CHAPTER 44

Today's mini magnum opus describes adventures in cell phone boosting. I figured after losing nearly every call I received yesterday and for a number of days prior, I had better wait on baking new muffins, researching the sawmill, and painting. Not that the painting thing had me too upset but I do need to be able to finish a conversation without ghosts interfering. I asked a few learned folk what they had learned about these things. Apparently, they are the cat's wee backside. Capable of leaping tall buildings and an outhouse or two in a single bound, they also magnify your sound and hang onto your calls. I wonder if the ghosts have these, for when they get calls from beyond?

Can you just hear it? "I'm talking to YOU" at about 150 decibels. They sound like they have one when they're in my attic.

In my research over several hours, I came across the information below on a website where we can do curb-side pick-up and the same information on one where we order things like replacement electrical cords for laptops. In trying to figure out just which booster might be the right one, I read the following:

*"4. The outdoor antenna need to install on the place where signal is good normally more than 3–4 bars."*

Three or four bars in one day is a good field trip in Florida. There wouldn't be any kind of signals happening after that, except maybe flagging down the Uber.

*"5. The outdoor antenna straight line from the repeater to 7 meters to avoid self-excitation."*

If your antenna self repeated at seven (7) meters, I would think self-excitation would be the least of your problems.

At a loss, I gave up.

How are some things so difficult and others just hard to manage? I got no answers, no understanding, no glimmer on how to figure it out. Of course, after four bars and a repeater, my indoor/outdoor antenna quit and now is off applying for the government benefit.

# CHAPTER 45

Coffee challenged, weather frustrated and don't talk to the shed. I have a few more signal things to try. Today's lesson in abject scorn is titled tv cabinet #2 and I thought I was going to need Lysol toting bees. I was excited, as the cable company came through with coax cable and connectors for seven bucks. Excellent service and picked it up this afternoon outside their door. They even had extra ideas on signal strength, too.

After I grabbed it and came back, I had some work to do online and my phone calls only faded a few times. Could cold air make it better? It didn't make me better with single milk coffee, double socks, and triple shirts. Thank god for seat heaters.

Sunny snow showers with a side of blizzard.

Are we living at Dairy Queen? While I was marvelling at this latest twist of Canadian weather to befall us, I was doing a lot of writing and some work, and getting ready for Friday night online trivia with Camp Big Canoe Camp Everywhere. Eight pm and we were revving up. I don't know why I was excited; last week I came in 44th out of forty-five players. With scores like that, I shouldn't have to try at all. Online laptop for the Zoom and on the phone for the scoring. A real tech geek, that's me. Watch me go! I'm crawling up the leader board from 44th to 17th place when suddenly I heard a series of beeps. I looked down and I realized they were coming from the laptop in my lap. Then the laptop decided it didn't want to play. Anything. Anymore. It crashed, went dark, hot and quit. Warm and frozen. You could've heard me without needing a signal booster. All my everything is on that thing. I was suddenly out of the game, in more ways than one. What in the freakin' dang world am I gonna do now?

# CHAPTER 46

Hello out there, I'm back on the air! Woohoo, who knew?

It turned out to be a whirlwind of a day in the Hundred Acre Wood. The blustery day gave way to sunshine and lollypops and all manner of lovely things, full of surprises and wonder. Aside from the snow, sleet, hail, and everything else that mail carriers are expected to wade through.

I received a call today from my cousin A, who had read the story already and couldn't believe it either. We looked at each other on the video call, shaking our heads. "WTF??" she asked. I said I had asked that, too, a number of times. As noted by another good friend, you can't make this up. Throughout the early morning, I had received a lot of super suggestions from folks on what to do and how to help my labyrinth of laptop woes. I had tried what ones I could and sadly, none of them worked. A said, "I was wondering what to do for your big birthday and I've decided this is what I'm doing." After much discussion and naysay from myself, she would not take nay for an answer and not one, but two wonderful, marvelous gift cards for Best Buy appeared in my in-box. Her daughter, Mic, helped too. A note was supposed to read "To my honorable cousin," but autocorrect working at its finest, it read "To My Horrible Cousin." I just roared. My mother always called folks horrible when they weren't being quite nice. I was overwhelmed and speechless by this beautiful, thoughtful gift. I continued my research into what was available, when and where. Promptly, the flyer for BB came up and I found several devices on sale right now, at our local BB in Peterborough. One was quickly ordered for pick-up. Within ten minutes, I received another email indicating my order was ready for pick-up! I could not believe it. Toilet paper, Lysol, and flour, take that!

I quickly headed out for Peterborough, watching my oft-leaded foot carefully. I arrived, there was no line, I was served, tapped, and gone within about ten minutes. I had also called Maars Music in Peterborough, thanks to my daughter, who advised me they are also a local Apple outlet, to ask about data recovery on the old one. It won't start now and when it did just once this morning, the blue screen of death was evident. I didn't realize it but BB sends your old device out; it is gone for quite a length of time before it's returned with no guarantee of help. Fair enough; they don't know 'til they look whether things are salvageable. Maars called me back, saying they were there, and to bring it on by on my way home. I hurried over, in case they were gone when I got there (this is me, after all) and no, they were still there, waiting for me, the last customer of the day. They looked at the burnt offering, felt it was unrepairable; however, they could retrieve the data and it would be on an external hard drive, most likely by Monday afternoon, if I'd care to return to pick it up. Well. I nearly fell over with gratitude and thanks. There's a lot of information on there that I'd love to have back, if at all possible. I skipped out of there with wings on my feet and sun in my heart.

I have to say now, right here, I am so thankful for friends and family. I don't know what I would do without all of you, sharing this journey of barely describable wilderness with me. Thank you, thank you, thank you.

Thanks to the vagaries of autocorrect, to my honourable cousin, I give a horrible mention of thanks, gratitude, and love. Could not do it without you, girlfriend.

# CHAPTER 47

Hello! Heather here from Radio M.A.C., coming to you live from KB, Ontario. Mac, no melted cheese, function, no fail! I hope your day before this one was as fun-a-day as you could make it. Maybe your weather was better than mine. No option for social distance visits outside at 32 degrees F, rain with an option of big white drops most of the day. May, you say . . .

I had thought, being Mother's Day, I would visit mine. She left us in 2009 but I have visited every special Sunday since, and more often, to update the folks on the happenings in life and to feel closer, at least for those moments, to what was. No go. All cemeteries were closed today, I would imagine fearing an influx of visitors wanting to be just like me. My gawd, do they know me? I'm thinking that's the last thing they'd want. The flying monkeys got out years ago and have been making my life a living hell ever since. The Wicked Witch of The North needs to step in and drop a house on them. I know of one available.

I needed to see my other mom so I did a porch drop of potted pansies and hellos and felt much better for having clapped eyes on both my eight-five-year-old ex-mom and dad. At least we could distance chat. Haven't hugged them since January, and like so many, it will be an epic hug of huge propor-tions when it finally happens. Same with kids. I'm thankful for FaceTime but . . . It was still so good to see faces, talk to family.

Still too cold to paint porch ceilings, it's time to get this office area fin-ished. The Mac is biding its perfect time, waiting for its fried, much older buddy to return. Maybe today. . . could my tenuous "good luck" hold?

# CHAPTER 48

It turned out to be a banner day in the hood. I've been trying to sort this office set up. I need to move furniture. Again. Of course, as always, nothing is too easy by the big breezy bay. Today, however, brings my good luck streak up to two. Two calls, two orders, two pick-ups. I have been fussing over the office organizing and today ordered some furniture assistive maneuver movers. I also got more paint assistive devices. I could use the tape over my mouth if it doesn't go well.

So, with the first order to my local hardware store, it was ready for pick up within the half hour. Wow! I was impressed. I know how busy all the stores are. No sooner had I hung up than my phone rang with the news that the laptop data was recovered and I could pick it up. Woohoo and wow! Off I roared in a flurry of road dust and expectations. I got to my small town and the order was ready, all protocols observed, then I headed out of town to the next bigger town to grab the offending article and new hard drive. I arrived just before closing once again, and it was all in order, disinfected, and ready to go! Double woohoo!

This was about three hours of driving by the time I got home so I'm now having a cuppa and figuring out how to hook the thing up and "migrate" the data. I should be good at that, I've been migrating all over the place for about half a century. More recently, kitchen to bath, bath to bed, bed to shed . . . watch that last one. Fraught with veritable opportunities for mayhem. Steel toe slippers required. Logging in and migrating. I can hear them all out there . . . migrating . . . bunkie to shed, shed to dudes, dudes to car . . . uh oh. This could require more than just coffee . . .

# CHAPTER 49

Please, dear god, send some warmth. Yesterday, I put my long, cozy, get-warm-over-everything sweater on the heat stove to warm it up. I told you before, no judging. I'm a wuss. I finally realized what the funny smell was about ten minutes later . . . the plastic melty-type threads were becoming cheesy without the Mac . . . Gawd, I just need some sun that's not full of white crap.

Today was epic use of the hard drive, in several instances. The data happily migrated from B to A, onto the laptop; however, who knew that Microsoft Office did not do the return trip as well? It's all there, waiting on the "B" side, to be flipped over when the needle gets to the big part at the end. Nothing but that crackly, sss sss sss—nada. I think the "A" side might've been a flop.

Maybe the DJ will play both sides without another phone call. I cannot get the data from B to A, nor the programs. It is worthy of a big phone call tomorrow. Meanwhile, I was emailing attachments to myself that I needed for today's paperwork adventures, only to find I can download them to the drive but not as a Word document. Ugh! "View only" and they want a subscription to a new Office program for a paltry $80 per year. Not bloody likely, says I. You knew the good luck had to come to a screeching, grinding halt, didn't you?

In other news, I got the furniture assistive mover maneuverer out and going. Ok, that damn piano was arguing with the little slidey do dahs and didn't want to go where I wanted to send it. Pianos are like that. Some have a grand outlook, others more upright in their view of their rightful place in society. Or at least the living room wall. I shoved, wiggled, pushed, and then I got to moving the thing. It slid beautifully sideways, until I wanted it to go a different direction. Story of my life. Sideways then downhill. I almost feel like Rodney Dangerfield. The cabinet and two pieces of the huge three-piece sectional were easier. The piece with the pullout bed got left where it was. The piano was still grumbling about running into it, so, much like Spring 020, they are both still in time out. The other two pieces slid like a flying saucer down a ski hill. Perfect landing and no casualties. Printer stand, table chair, tv and cords, all thankfully, ok.

Later that same day, I could be found sitting on sectional A, waiting for the B side and strumming a "C" chord while I waited for the denouement of my day. Look it up.

# CHAPTER 50

Fifty Shades of Disbelief. Fifty times I've shared the shite and shinola of my days since returning from the southlands. A veritable vestige of visible confusion, in other words, a mess. Thanks to all of you for tuning in.

Some things have been brighter than others . . . lovely gifts, all the good wishes, thoughts, and ideas from all of you. Some, not so much . . . bad weather, laptop crashing, terrible weather, Newman up above . . . did I mention the weather?

Most of the time, it's good. I mean, actually, it's ridiculous, who else camps out in their own house? Ya I know, when I looked around, I didn't see anybody else either. Still working on fixing programs and the mercury is finally creeping up so there may be painting soon.

Fifty Ways to Move Your TV. Or, is that move it fifty times in one day? Either or both hurt my back.

Today's migrating mishap involved a heat stove. It would not start up this morning and as has been oft repeated, it's cold outside and I'm a heat wuss. The long, cozy, get-warm-over-everything sweater was not going on there because it wouldn't get warm, never mind melt. I had called the people and noted that one stove sounded like a 747 taking off, complete with in-flight safety demonstration, while the other just needed regular service. This morning featured the upgraded program, which included breakfast and a movie with a side of "not working at all." When my chilly self comes out in the morning, I don't want to freeze while I'm waiting for my coffee. I quickly emailed the propane folks and shared my plight. I had also asked for delivery after checking to see one tank was at 0 percent and the other at 15 percent. A bit low for these frigid times, not to mention the barbeque days ahead. When the timely delivery arrived, the #2 blast furnace still had not kicked in. No liftoff while delivery dude was here, either. Back to the drawing board. Before I sat to write another email, I tried the age-old remedy of jiggle the handle, or in this case, the cord. Damn if it didn't start up right away! Newman, you black and white little bugger . . . The cord . . . I'm thinking another service call could be in order . . . maybe they can send the exorcist . . .

# CHAPTER 51

Rampart, Station 51 . . .

Memories . . .

I had my own Station 51 here with the Apollo stove and the constant frustration of furniture. I decided to try again to move sofa slidey and downhill piano. No comment from Snow and the Very Heavy Seven. I think they're having coffee with the shed and the bunkie has interrupted with breaking news. Breaking my back, I think, is the news. Lazy sods. The sofa still had blue sliders under it. I could not believe how easily it slid across the room, once I got the table and piano bench out of the way. The piano actually did what it was told this time, and slid to where it will now live for all eternity. Or, at least 'til it decides it would make better music somewhere else. I now know the meaning of "make your own kind of music, sing your own special song." I know you sang that; I heard you.

The piano seems happy where it has landed. The sofa piece is settled where it will now belong, too. I think the tv cabinet, from its exalted place across the room, has surveyed the scene and declared it acceptable. Now I can see it from here and look to there. The office is taking shape, too. The brightness factor is good, for someone like me who needs sun and light and all things happy. It was suggested by a friend yesterday that I should move to Florida. I am thinking there is some truth to that, since sunshine and bright skies are good for all of us, especially right now. However, those pesky little things called citizenship and healthcare get in the way.

The next thing to tackle is the dining room. The 358 pairs of salt and peppers need their home and their cabinet. Oh, but wait . . . that cabinet is somewhere out there . . . storage A or storage B . . . not sure which door it's behind but Monty has not been much help thus far. How come I never win the car or the trip to Tahiti?

# CHAPTER 52

Fifty-two . . . so many meanings . . . the number of cards in a deck that you have to pick up when you drop them; folks from the Regent Park hood of my youth remember it as the local police station, as I recall. There are that many weeks in a year and from numerology, we have the explanation that the number "52 is a number of introspection, mental acuity, and expression of personal freedom." Well, who knew? All this fiddle faddle I'm spewing every day means I'm mentally acute? Maybe that's only today . . .

It also leads me to share what I found during today's digging and slogging foray. A foray of mini proportions, it was, as the weather was rainy and the trek was not star-filled with William Shatner waiting on the end of a communicator. "Ouija" the board. Or, as my young nephew called it, "The Family Ghost Game." Maybe Newman heard about that somewhere and found it first. That must be how the shed and the car are in cahoots with the chick and the seven dudes . . .

We used to play this after family dinners, Christmas night (that explains a multitude of psychological issues), and just sometimes when there were a few of us around. My sister and I both had an affinity for it, being blessed, or cursed, as the case may be, with the "Scottish sight." Visions of many things that were not sugar plums danced in our heads, sometimes later they happened, sometimes not, but mostly it was fun. Except the time the ghost must've come in the little bedroom in the back of the house where my daughter had woken up from her nap and she asked from her crib why the curtains were blowing as she told us of the delightful chat she was having with the old lady in her room. Right away, the game was put away back in the box and the box put out with the tools. We did, however, keep the kid. This was another house but the number was 52 . . .

This house appears to be haunted all by itself, or maybe it's just me who is haunted . . . A lovely virtual happy hour tribal visit, followed by Camp Big Canoe Trivia. I'm the only one who can play online trivia and come 45th out of forty-four players . . .

I'm thinking that kind of karma is inescapable.


# CHAPTER 53


I had a different day yesterday. No, there was no Ouija involved! If you ask the Shed, there might've been but we aren't talking just now. I was unpacking boxes and none of those outdoor edifices lifted a finger. Even those dudes with the dudette, nada. I think I would've even been thankful to see Newman. Ok. Maybe not. I had moved a cardboard ocean onto the back deck and since it was Finally Sunny, I got at it. I know I should've painted but it's going to rain tomorrow. And the next day. Amazing, the flotsam and jetsam you have in your life. You might sense a theme or continuous thought here.

Fahoo forays, dahoo dorays.

Christmas has always played a huge part in my life. Whether I'm freezing in the summer home or cozy warm in the winter home, it doesn't keep Christmas from coming; it comes, just the same. I'm as perplexed as the Grinch is about it all.

Today's experiences continued with more dishes, and cookware, and everything but spoons. No muffin pans or button pants or chocolate macaroons. I think the dishes and Corningware were happy to be liberated, and the huge pile of newspaper, all but obliterated.

# CHAPTER 54

Car 54, where are you? According to numerology, fifty-four means "shall live forever and will not die." Oh my god. You mean I'm dealing with the house, shed, bunkie and seven dudes with attitude until the end of time? Or those magical words "For Sale" appear suddenly on the front lawn in the dark of night . . . oh no, I'm having way too much fun . . . it's a good threat to those misbehaving miscreants. It's camping in place as usual and carry on, keeping a physical distance from almost everything I own.

Since the sun did shine, the grass has riz, I wonder where the flowers is?

They are outside, in the bunkie, by the deck and in the washing well. Sounds like a Clue game. Colonel Mustard, with a spoon, in the shed. By the time I find them, the pattern will be decades out of date and unrecognizable. The shed snickers quietly to itself in the morning mist. To the flowers, Batman. I found my pots and baskets, not hard when they're out there staring at me with reproach. Gardening gloves, not so much. I'm almost afraid to look. Any thoughts on substitute gloves? Dog poop bags? Too slippery. Then there's that constant rip off the roll for a new one. Ziplock bags? The sandwich size, not the snack size. Large freezer size? Too hard to close them all just enough on your arm. Welding gloves? I could look like a knight going off to war. It's only a shed, apparently. I went commando hands and what a scrub mess after, but was it ever nice to play in the dirt. Results are good, too. I guess I can still plant flowers; at least they have a good chance of staying where they belong.

# CHAPTER 55

As this had been a busy few days, I decided to devote some time to research and learning things, as promised earlier.

The area here, as noted in a prior post, was a sawmill for many years and then was divided into forty-six original cottage lots, which were sold to families and/or rented for the summer. Just down the lake from Pleasant Point, retirement home area of former premier, Leslie Frost, and across from Sturgeon Point, an early affluent area of summer residents, our little inlet has been the quiet sibling to its more prominent family members since it began. Originally known as Tweedie's Bay, later changed to Kennedy after the landowners, it has seen much change and progress. There is a hill to the south which places our little community in a hollow facing the lake. On this hill, buried in the brush of another large old family holding, was a log cabin, which was the forerunner of my cottage. Lived in by the family who farmed the land, the path from the cabin came down the hill, through my neighbour's yard, and ended beside my house in front of the lake. Traces are still visible if you look closely. When logging was no longer profitable and becoming more futile with the increase of cottaging and pleasure boats on the lake, my cottage, a tiny storey and a half cabin, was built, followed by the store and post office. The rest of the park, which we have use of with our cottage fees, was donated by the family at a later date. Originally, there was just a small right of way down to the pier, for the cottagers to use. This park is directly across from my house and I am lucky enough to have one of the best views around. My small cabin was raised and a large addition added in 1973 when the prior owners purchased it from the last of the farm family and made it their home. It also became a central gathering place of the cottage families at the Bay, by all accounts, so I seem to fit in nicely. According to several neighbours, it is haunted. By who or what, they aren't sure. I did suggest that they try camping in place here for a night or two so they could find out!

# CHAPTER 56

Today was a banner day. Today, I snagged (read it again) not one but two plumbers. The original dudes who have done the plumbing for me at several homes over the years and a new guy plumber, recommended. Both for quotes. That sumptuous pump you may have heard tell of requires a partner in crime and a different set up and some fancy dancy wiring updates. When your microwave goes on and your sumpy pump goes off, you've got some kind of problem going on. And off. The power bar blues. The pump is sharing a bar stool with the hot water heater. It has all the making of disaster. And that wispy cord snaking up through the trap door . . . If the shed gets involved, it's game over.

So, several quotes will be forthcoming on that. It's a good 'hood when you can take a walk, talk to the plumber dude when he comes out of somebody's yard and says yup, know about it, and will stop by when he's done. And does. New dude remains to be seen. He's supposed to be seen tomorrow afternoon after pm so here's hoping he is. I'm not sure what the new updates are for businesses that come to your house, but we'll follow the protocols and hope he can do what he needs to do. Somebody has to. I cannot have another cellar tsunami like before.

The other good part was more tidying. And unpacking. And putting away. And virtual happy hour. And sunsets. Gotta love 'em.

The sad thing was the announcement that there would be no overnight summer camp this summer. We kind of knew, figured, thought it was coming but sad all around when it happens. So many kids of all ages look forward to their summer sessions. These times we are all going through are affecting so many things, events, happenings for so, so many of us. All we can do is try to stay well, be safe, and keep doing what we're doing.

# CHAPTER 57

Thank the ever-lovin' lord for sunshine. The best thing ever during this time of distance and solitude. Sun, water, and sand. I might think I'm back south but the weather in On-tari-ari-ario is just fine right now. Plumber #1 arrived, complete with Darth Vader mask and boot covers and gave me quite a reasonable quote for the work required below stairs in the built-in pool. I wonder if Moses had this problem? If you want to part the waters, or even make them go away, just ask. Awaiting Plumber #2. Hope he didn't forget!

Today was grass day at the Bay. Socially distant golf carts were the order of the day. Since the sun shone, the lawnmowers ran! Everybody's cuttin' turf today; saw every vehicle known to man.

ATV's, a few cars, dogs, and one squirrel all respecting the distance and talking up a storm from afar. The squirrel was the worst though . . . Scrabbling around in the yard, on the deck. Apparently, they like recycling. As long as they don't like it in the kitchen, I'm good. The social part was huge today. With the warm weather and sunshine, I'm thinking everyone is getting cabin fever. I had a distant BYOB happy hour drink of my own with my neighbour, S, around the corner then this evening, another online happy hour with my camp peeps. I did, however, manage dinner in-between. Funny thing, though. Fairly often throughout the call, we would hear screeching, squawking, squealing coming down the line. After a couple minutes I realize they're all looking at me with great expectation. What? I say. "Is it Newman?" they ask. Or somebody else? Ahah! It's the shed . . . everybody's in cahoots! Great laughter ensues from various locales across Southern Ontario. I hang my head. Why would they all be blaming me??? Laugh, laugh, my pretties, just wait 'til the day comes when we can all be together again. Bwahahah! I shake my head. Note to Self: Never tell the besties about the beasties. They will never let you live it down.

Keep distant and wash yer hands, just make sure you put your drink down first.

# CHAPTER 58

A different take on things today. Who knew facial recognition doesn't work with a mask?

Many questions, the gift of a cloth mask along with many more questions, awaited me this morning as I arrived at our local hospital for a non-routine test. Experiencing discomfort and pain, late last week, I was fast tracked through online healthcare and scheduled as quickly as possible. I couldn't have asked for better or more timely service from our frontline staff.

As I sit here awaiting information, I'm reflecting on the number of times I've been here with all the others. Parents, husband, other family, and good friends. Suddenly, I'm in the other chair and by myself. These times don't allow for anybody to come with you. You come through the door, alone. Down the hall and into reception, where I answer the same questions and then sit, everyone distant from the others, waiting. Finally, it's time.

I had found a lump and a sore. With no doctor on the end of the phone that day, I called online. Very quickly, I was assessed and given an appointment time within several hours. That appointment led to a referral for tests and a follow up with my own doctor on Tuesday. Today is Thursday. A very quick turnaround in any time but during a lockdown, incredible. I had been told that all required doctors would be there and all results would be given right then, if anything further was needed, it would be done as well. Phenomenal. I have nothing but praise, thanks and respect for all of these dedicated and hardworking people. The relief I felt when I was told I was fine, unbelievable. When I was told the lump was normal due to age, well, you can imagine.

Age. So many things are related to it. The grey hair I can't cut, the sore muscles from moving furniture, and the fact that sleep evades my nights more often than it should. All of these shrink like a balloon in a freezer when faced with health issues. No health, no balloons.

Of course, in my world, no good news goes unpunished. I came home to rest and relax and as I sat with my lemon tea, heaving a huge sigh of relief, I heard a noise. I looked up and around, listening again and there it was. Newman. Noooooooooo!

# CHAPTER 59

I hope if it is your weekend that it is glorious and relaxing, that you have lots of wonderful things planned, that you go . . . Never mind. Stick to changing your PJs when you change the coffee filter and you'll be fine.

Lest you think things be calm and collected around here after yesterday, Think Again. With the Latest Adventures of Newman just waiting for an encore, the night was rough. Every noise, shudder, wind whisper was his, whether it was or not. Growing up, every time there was a noise, my dad always said, "It's just the house settling." As my mother rather dryly replied one time, "We've been here thirty years, don't you think it's settled by now?" I don't think Newman, old pal, old buddy had been here for thirty minutes before I was hearing things. I was the one not settled. The pesty dudes have me scheduled for Monday or sooner on a cancellation and this afternoon, my wonderful neighbour, F, decided he needed some chainsaw practice and since he's been eyeing it for some time, suggested he do so on the tree on the side of my house. This tree is taller than the house and weaves its many threads through the old tv tower, complete with a huge impressive-looking router on top, up over the roofline, past the satellite dish and to the sky beyond. I think signals from Mars could've come through if they weren't blocked by foliage. Maybe the first guys in space said, "KBay, we've got a problem, Houston's not answering." Which came first, the tower or the tree? I mean, would you plant a tree there in the tower or put your tower over the tree? It done boggles the mind. Since the tree has to be thirty or more years young, you have to wonder. I wonder if this antenna ever doubled as a ladder during times of extreme neighbourhood hide and seek? He cut and I dragged at a distance and we got a good chunk of it cut away. Even after the noise, dragging and hauling, you could still hear the scrabbling and scruffling of each little hoof, or paw . . . or . . .

# CHAPTER 60

I was asked to do the Call to Worship for virtual church for this Sunday. So, if you're inclined, you can sign in to St Andrews Church, Lindsay, ON, on Facebook or YouTube and see the service. Also, having online coffee hour at 11:15!

Yesterday was a different day. The chosen mom and dad, Papa & Grandma, were doing some isolated gardening at their beautiful home about a twenty-minute drive away. As a break from Newman, et al, I driveway-dropped a tree and some ferns for the fam. The things you do for love ♥. I donned my new mask, which I had washed, and sallied forth. I couldn't help but wonder a bit, though, about the ear elastic. I think somebody's Day of the Weeks are sagging down around their knees out there. It was good to lay eyes on the family and have virtual hugs. Did my part for the tree hole too . . . some folks are taking them out, some putting them back in. Too bad we couldn't swap a deal . . . no extra charge for the tv tower.

They said no.

Bonus—Newman?

Still no. Some folks just don't know how to have fun.

They were able to have a good FaceTime with granddaughter, M, as well, though. Priceless!

Epistle #60, with 60 the number representing family, home, and nurturing. Now I'm laughing, loudly and at great length. Nobody told my upstairs neighbour this was supposed to be all about home. Nurturing. The family part, I've got that nailed. The home?? Hahaha!

For a change of pace, maybe it's time I actually tried to take The Lake. I hear you out there. It is a rallying cry. The snow from last week has melted, what's taking you so long? When I got back, the heat was huge! Not complaining, mind you. Just a small dip. It could go with those mini chips. Oh my . . . chicken like I was six and seven again. Nope, too cold. Those kids who were in earlier—nuts, all of them. Their parents need to get them psychological intervention before it's too late. Or maybe it's me who needs it. Freakin' freezing! Of course, I remember my eight-and-a-half-year-old self turning blue, shaking with frozen delight in the Mays and Junes of my youth. I grew up to be a lifeguard, too, can't ya tell? Now, fahgeddaboutit. Of course, as soon as I was back, the house silent, I Heard It Again! I could've wept. Cannot believe it. C'mon Monday!

Maybe I'll just sleep in the bunkie . . . it can't be as cold as the lake, of course, there is that tree tangled in the clothesline pole . . .

# CHAPTER 61

The day after Sunday, usually referred to as Monday, unless you're in a living, breathing Ground Hog Day, then it's just déjà vu all over again. I'm thinking I'm not the only one feeling this way. Wake up, post the day's musings, get up, coffee & pjs in the sun and maybe get dressed by noon. In clean pjs, what kind of a girl do you think I am? Ha. I heard you. Shrink on speed dial, right beside the plumber, electrician, pest guy, neighbour with extra-large chain saw . . .

The car and shed are laughing, the bunkie is telling them how the attic dude is still there and it will soon be time for round three, just wait for it.

I tried, today, to put a few more things away. Folded the foldable, stacked the stackable, and realized I had nowhere for the folded and stacked to go. I thought maybe I'd try to rig more shelves, however, that was an exercise in futility. I visited the bunkie, that den of skeptical iniquity and discovered a small shelf unit out there that I can bring in to use. I think it's soon going to be time to rent a truck and grab my crap. It's physically distanced all over the southern reaches of the northern hemisphere and I'm getting damn tired of it. If you've ever tried camping in place in your own house, while *Mutual of Omaha's Wild Kingdom* tries to film a 36th season in your attic, you'll know what I mean. It's not the fact that the stuff isn't here, although that's bad enough. It's that I can't get it even if I could figure out exactly which place it is in. I know movers are considered essential services but what they would charge me for the dubious honour is dubious. I think. Maybe it needs a phone call.

To get it there was $1,200 plus an additional two rental trucks at $150 plus $225 each plus gas and food. Now, if you subtract the piano and venerable tv cabinet which you have all been introduced to, and which were already professionally returned last fall, I'm left with approximately $430.00 plus one truck and some help. Hmmmm. Might be doable. Take out the professionals, more doable. Pay-a-kid and one truck, $168.95 plus pizza and one face mask. Now, we're talking. This just might be a happening. Monday Funday could take on a whole new meaning. I think maybe Wednesday Sense Day. It has a nice ring to it. Don't tell any of the damn buildings, they could kibosh the whole thing.

# CHAPTER 62

Not a good day so far. Here I sit, outside, listening to scrabbling dudes in the attic eaves. I'm not sure if it's bird, a plane . . . the only thing I know is it's not Superman. It could be Super Squirrel, Jesus. I am waiting, not so patiently, for pesty dudes. I have already called and asked them to put a rush on it. I even recorded the noise. Not a beautiful noise, sorry Neil Diamond, just a damn racket.

I am thinking that the ingress needs to be found, an egress forced, and the outlet sealed. Right frigging now. The good news is at least they sound like they're in the eves rather than the ceiling . . . but how did they get in? The sixty-four-thousand-dollar question. At today's values, since that show came out in 1941, it would be the $1,059,121.95 question, courtesy of the Martha Stewart of Shelving. Helluvan upgrade. What is a downgrade, however, is the fact that the little buggers are still in there. I am sitting outside here and I can hear it or them running around the eaves, up and down, like they are outside for recess. I wonder what the classroom entails . . .

"Now listen up, boys and girls." This is how we chew through the wall . . . the wires . . . the drywall . . . the wood siding . . . No, Gertrude, you're not chewing hard enough; you need to break through that truss so all the goodies fall down onto her head . . ." Ugh.

I am beyond fed up. The attic neighbours are not adhering to the terms of the lease and need to be evicted. Too bad I can't turn off the heat . . .

In other better news, the plumber is coming June 3 to fix the sumptuous pump. I wonder if he has a sideline in insidious rodents?

The other good news is I found one of my dressers . . . phew! If you look hard enough. . . I now need to put it together. That shed is feeling bad, I know it is. Maybe I'll find some spoons in the drawer. But what's this?? Drum sticks and a kick pedal . . . oh my god. I know where the drums are. Maybe I can set up the family band and socially distance the hell out of the resident rodents.

It's worth a try . . .

# CHAPTER 63

An interesting one today. I'll tell you all about it. If you're still reading, you must be a regular! Maybe you're a double double. Either way, listen up!

So, to continue from yesterday's erstwhile tale of the Tale of Tails, we rejoin our heroine as she awaits the arrival of the pesty dudes, once more. The tap dancing of each hoof/paw/foot has been heard extensively and at great length and I've about had enough. Our hero arrives toting all manner of rodent 'radicatin' paraphernalia. First of all, the noise didn't go away with the rising of the sun. So, they or it never sleeps. Day or night. Consequently, neither do I. I'm about done in with the heat, (not whining) exhaustion, and the inability to locate my fans . . . oh wait, all six of you are already here. But I digress.

The kitchen wall was where it was found. This time. Noises above and noises below, there was no silence by the lake today. It seems, after taking a wall outlet off and turning off the power, inserting a camera and making popcorn, the movie shows a little baby red squirrel in between the wall trusses by the floor. Then, the paneling has to come off, then a hole made so he can fish the little so and so outta there. What a cute little beast, as long as it is not in your wall. He manages to snag him through the hole. I'm outside, at a distance. Apparently, this is a good news/bad news story. As soon as he grabs this one, he hears another one, the next stud over. Ugh! Same routine: camera, paneling, revealing not one, but two more in there. Squawking like somebody stole their toys. Or at least their mother. Double ugh.

By this point, it's pretty obvious (to the pesty dude) that Mama has left the building and can't get back in for the kids. There has been a black squirrel out there (remember the hair in the vent) but it wasn't red. Local knowledge tells me red squirrels are not black. Who knew?

After considerable arseing (Canuck word) around, number three is snagged and bagged and removal complete. Off to the wilds of the back of the backyard where, hopefully, Mama will find them and they'll all bugger off for parts unknown. Unknown to me, by me, far from me. It's so little to ask at this point in the game, isn't it? Repair and replace the holes and paneling and, oh my god, a silent wall as good as 1974 when it was built. I hope and I pray that it remains silent.

Since it was 32C/94F degrees by the time this was all done, I decided to run to town quickly and do drive through ice cream for supper. No judging. All my button pants are still packed and it's too hot to cook. A quick side of Fans for Sale at the GT Boutique and it really is summer now! Let's hope the critters take their holidays somewhere else and keep isolated since they've finished their quarantine here.

# CHAPTER 64

A peaceful night in ole KBay followed by lovely morning coffee. Who knew it could happen? I am ever thankful to pesty dude for enforcing the evictions. One more night of peaceful slumber and I might be human again. Not sane, nobody can be expecting that, human will do.

Let me tell you about a time when it was more sane and lots more fun. Oh wait, you'd be reading about somebody else. Today was finally unload the bunkie and find missing treasures day but that's nearly every day. Pinkie & The Brain have got nothing on me! You'll never guess what I found. Nope. Nope. Not that either. Ha!

There are now boxes on the deck where people could sit if you were allowed to. Right now, it's home to scrapbooks and photo albums and pottery and Christmas lights and. . . one box containing loaf pans. I freakin' kid you not. Mini, but nevertheless, loaf pans. Aarrgghh! Oh, I'm so sad it's too hot to bake . . .

I also found a sign.

"Sometimes I open my mouth and my mother comes out."

Is that not the truth? My mom used to say the darnedest things and you thought it was kids.

Early morning: "It would be warm if it wasn't so cool out."

The evening after bad weather: "The sun comes up in time to go down."

My favourite: unnamed Christmas décor—"Christmas what-the-hells."

I found several what-the-hells in my digging. A wreath that could double as a floor polisher. A box of lights that could shine brighter if they worked when you plugged them in. See, my mother is still here. One more thing I found today. My family crest. My family on Mom's side were from Scotland, emigrating in the early 1900s/1920s from Aberdeen and Glasgow. The Shepherd motto: "*Dextra Cruce Vincit*—My right hand conquers by the Cross." Surprise: not about sheep. My grandfather Shepherd came by ship ninety-five years ago, in 1925, to Montreal then out west to work on a farm for six months (possibly to help pay his passage), then to the promised land of Toronto. His uncle before him had suggested he follow him there as it was a wonderful land of opportunity. He worked for York Township Hydro for his career 'til he passed in 1965 of long term heart issues. I was five. I used to call him when we got home after every visit if I saw a street light out and he told me he'd fix it the next day ☺. Sweet memory. My crest can now join the history wall of the house as I continue to make my own history here.

# CHAPTER 65

A busy one, a wet one, a lot going on one!

Moving, finding, and putting. Today was also the day my first pension cheque arrived. Holy crapadoodle! Another "oh my gawd." I'm now officially older. Sixty years young. I figured it was fitting that it arrived on the 65th story. Fitting, too, that yesterday I find that sign about hearing your mother's voice out of your own mouth. "Better take that pension early, you know, they might run out." Holy jeez, what would she make of what's going on right now? I can't ask her, I can't get in there. I think I'm getting old. A pension. Some kind of right of passage, isn't it? I have Arrived. Arrived at the doctor, the chiropractor, the hospital, the mental therapist. The bungalow state of life. You don't want stairs because you don't want to climb them anymore; you forget what you went up there for anyway. You want everything on one floor in your life so you don't have to hunt up and down for stuff. I'm the wrong person to be talking about that one. I think I'm too old now to be chasing my belongings all over parts known or unknown. Even might've known. I got a pension that says so! And today, my fine captives of reality, is the day I go gather my stuff. The truck is booked, the distancing in place, masks ready, and it's time to gather. Very fitting on pension day. Kind of an assembling of all the life things. Get your stuff, we will now pay you to sit home and look at it!!!! Oh my, I can hardly even get that out. Does the government know what's been going on here? I mean, they must've been talking to all my buildings and the dudes let the cat out of the bag.

I can't wait to read tomorrow's wee warble to find out what happened on today's gathering gander. You just know something will. Oh. I'm the writer . . . oh yeah, forgot that part. Maybe the shed can tune us all in; after all, it'll be making room all day . . .

# CHAPTER 66

It was quite a day. I grabbed the truck this morning and set off down the road in our household replenishment adventure. About halfway there, I had a panic attack thinking I'd forgotten the key; however, there it was, right on my keychain. After I came back down to earth, we carried on, arriving at The Unit after a rattle-bang trip, the empty truck crying for a load all the way. Lugging and slugging, slinging and flinging, the Christmas tree, the frowning table. I guess this table was a source of amusement to the kids. My daughter could never figure out why it was so sad. The carving in the wood looks like frowning. I never knew! It didn't take much longer than an hour and everything was on and out of there! Except, of course, when we were almost out of there and I had to stop and find out if the floor pallets were ok to leave. No, you have to take them, they said. But someone else could use them, says I. Sorry. Back around we go, grumbling all the way about begging forgiveness instead of asking. After we've loaded them on and stacked them, one of the people there waiting chimed in with "I'll take them." Huge sigh. Back we go with our convoy of collected belongings and stop so we can unload the darn things. After that, it was Willy Nelson time, on the road again, we went. We had to have Kawartha Dairy ice cream for lunch, since we were going right by, it really would've been a sin not to stop. Oh, was that ever good in the heat. Best Salty Carmel Truffle and Moose Tracks stop evah!! Next stop in our cavalcade of collection, the other place where things are kept for me. Ya gotta love family.

Remember the horrible mention in the beautiful laptop gift? That sweet girl's cottage has the rest of the stuff stored in an unused area. I am so blessed and thankful. Another back breaker load of what could fit and one full fifteen foot U-Haul was ready to go. They handle well with a full load so I suppose we can be thankful for small mercies. Finally, we arrive in the driveway. Oh, my gawd, now the fun begins. You know around here, it's never easy. We start bringing things in and about twenty minutes later, the thunder starts and the skies open. We are soaked, boxes getting soaked and ice cream is a distant memory. We try to wait it out; however, it wins. Looking like a couple of shaggy dogs, we decide to finish in the early morning. The rain kept going until well into the evening, so hopefully it was a good call.

I can't quite believe how sore I'm feeling. I think I've done my last U-Haul adventure. At the risk of using the "O" word, as I did so often in the last story, I felt every one of those pensionable years.

# CHAPTER 67

The truck got emptied this morning by my wonderful daughter who arrived at 6:45 am, banging on the door and waking me up from a not-so-deep sleep on the couch where I had crashed last night in exhaustion, and we had it done by the time we poured the second cup! Well, I poured them. We took turns grabbing and so forth. Maintaining the distance! Have to remember that, especially when it's so easy to forget.

So, the truck was done, the house a mess, and I was kindly reminded it was a year to the day that we did this before, only the stuff was leaving. What a year it's been. Can't quite believe it. I seem to recall some Kawartha Dairy involved in those days, as well. Must be some kind of Heather Relocation Tradition. I am back, in my own wee hoose and moving forward. Somehow . . . first I have to find where forward is—I can't see it beyond the boxes and bins. That truck sat out there for sixteen hours and those dudes, the shed, the car—nobody lifted a finger! Ha. Just wait, you will get yours, my pretties.

## LATER THAT DAY . . .

I was moving, sorting, stacking and I heard sirens. Lots of sirens. It wasn't me!!! was all I could think. I look out to see a cavalcade of emergency vehicles roaring past my house, barely stopping at my sign and rushing up the road. There's not much left of the road after you pass my house so I couldn't figure out where they all thought they were going. Next thing, police, ambulance, then the huge fire trucks. All down here where we all know the names of all the dogs and everyone stops to see how you're doing. They have been spending more time at the end of my driveway lately, more than usual. Today, everyone was rushing past my driveway in the wake of half of the emergency services vehicles in the entire area. We find out that one of the neighbours down the block smelled smoke from his furnace. Apparently, all was fine; however, then I wanted to see them all try to get out of there. Time to make the popcorn. I needed a break, anyway. I'm glad there was no smoke at 9 am when I took the truck back; I'd never have gotten out of there.

While I was being one of many nosey neighbours, I spoke with my friend B, who passed along an old cookbook from the Lindsay I.O.D.E., 1953. Since she knew I was finding out many things about the area, she thought I would like it. I recognized many of the names, including one "Jean Tompkins." I had been speaking earlier this afternoon on the phone, as I often do, with Martha of the Shelves, and her mother was a Jean Tompkins. This morning, prior to the action movie outside my door, we had talked of recipes: cake, desserts, and loaves that her mother made many times in our youth. We are gathering recipes for a camp cookbook so it was fitting we spoke of these favourite ones. Lo and behold, within the cookbook I received this morning were the following: Sour Milk Chocolate Cake, Coronation Fruit Cake, and Nine Day Pickles, all courtesy of Jean along with a number by a Mary Tompkins. As far we are aware, she never lived in the area; however, as she was a prominent writer and cook and was very involved with the church. It's possible . . . but not likely. Karma, once again. There are Kennedys providing goody notes as well as Thomsons (who owned this house prior to me) and many other local family names. I'd love to hear more about these dedicated ladies who provided so many great culinary ideas from their combined experience.

# CHAPTER 68

I think it's morning. Maybe it's still the night before. Maybe we need to ask Mary Hartman . . . and maybe not. What's with frost overnight? Siberia?? It was a balmy 52 degrees today; just wait half an hour, it will change.

The first order of business: I realize that I have no cash. Is anybody using any these days? I didn't have any and my lovely neighbour, grass guy, has been for the weekly manicure of the estate. I'm glad something can get a manicure these days. But cash it is, so off to quickly grab some with wipes and sanitizer. I've been away so long, I didn't recognize the place. They've redecorated with new ATMs and copious amounts of plexiglass.

Next up, with the truck unloaded hither and thither, it's time to unpack as soon as I grab my long socks off the stove. I told you before, no judging.

The first bin I grab is labelled "Kitchen." I look around, just to make sure. Stove, fridge. Pretty safe bet it's in the right room and so am I. I take the lid off. When what, to my wondering eyes should appear . . . spoons.

Before we all get too excited, they are the hang on the wall kind, on a rack. In a tea emergency, they'd be fine. Grab 'n go! For practicality, they are sorely lacking, all ornate and silver and fancy doodah. But I couldn't stop laughing. Ha. First thing out of the box! I heard the shed grumbling. Dishes, glassware, then the good stuff. Wine glasses. Woohoo! And so forth. I need to step on it since the plumber dude is coming in a few days and he won't be able to find his way in here. Or out of here, for that matter.

As I forge on with this, because unpacking can be boring unless you're finding spoons and loaf pans in every box, I'll share another recipe page. Folks seemed to enjoy it. Tomorrow should be far more exciting, with plenty of opportunities for mishap and mayhem today. I hear the bunkie whispering to the car. Thanks for checking in!

# CHAPTER 69

Bit of a different take on things today. Sometimes, you just have to support. I have a good friend whose dad passed the other night of illness. She was there, without family support and alone. Her sister is compromised so was unable to help in any way. Then, my friend had to be tested for COVID 19 and await results, both for herself and her late father. Thankfully, negative in both cases. A group of us are close, some having known each for forty-odd years. We decided to do a fruit basket; however, during these COVID times, nowhere close was providing them. I went to the grocery store, appropriately masked and distant, and gathered all the things for the goody basket. Cheeses, crackers, snacks, tea, coffee, chocolate, munchies, wine, etc. Yummy stuff, enough to fill a box, never mind a basket. The point of this mini missive is to highlight goodness and kindness. I am a long-time shopper at this particular store; however, they wouldn't have known who I was since I was masked. The cashier commented on how someone was going to enjoy a lovely feast. I told her of our care package for our friend and what happened. She asked if I had a basket. I did, however, not as big as it needed to be. She called to the young man who works in the back, and he got the basket assembler. They told me to wait in my car, they'd be out. They took everything and created a beautiful box, wrapped and tied, for our friend, then brought it right out to my car and loaded it in the trunk. They also said anytime I'm doing something like that, to let them know. They are happy to help people who are helping others. I was so thankful and overwhelmed. It was not a huge thing nor a big undertaking, but that they were kind, thoughtful, and thankful to have a shopper appreciate what they're doing, touched me at a time when everything is difficult and uncertain. The casher told me they want to be part of good things happening.

I liked that. I want to be part of good things happening, too. I think we all need some Good Things Happening around us today. Thank you to Lindsay Valu Mart for all your help and concern for my friend and her family.

Let me know what Good Things are happening around you.

# CHAPTER 70

Today was a busy one. After yesterday's good feels and feeling good, I was glad to share it all with you.

Today, I was back at it in earnest. I keep mentioning Ernest, but he never shows up to work earnestly or even not at all. He must be buds with Grumpy, the dude. I have a deadline as the plumberdudes are showing up tomorrow and need distant access to plumbing things. That means I need to distance my stuff from the accesses. I was working away in here, up to my eyeballs in figurative alligators, when my phone went off, signaling a message. I know, it happens to all of us. I had my hands full with bins so I got to it a bit later. I find a message from my wonderful neighbour, J, who was giving me an electric fireplace, which will definitely help with heat in the older part of the house in the fall . . . or maybe even tomorrow. She said they'd be home in a few minutes if I wanted to see if I had a dolly, figure out where it would go, etc. I said, sure, I wanted a break from lugging and slugging anyway. It does get old, like me, after a while! (Ok, last old joke.) Just as I was finishing up what I was about, I heard a loud noise outside. A kind of scraping, thudding kind of noise. I went out to see and here lovely neighbour had already brought it over and it was sitting on my deck. Wow. No dolly required. I saw it out there, then looked down the hall and into the kitchen beyond . . . no way was that thing getting in here. The Jenga of Boxland has taken over and I'll never be seen again. So now, I figured I'd better get moving on that situation. I didn't want the thing sitting outside overnight. So, I put and placed and picked and unpacked and was able to make a path, get rid of boxes and bins and get the thing in the door. I ran with excitement, because, really, that's the only way to run. Nobody says they run with dread and horror in their hearts, well, only if they're in an old late-night thriller that came on well after Johnny

Carson was over, Nurse Ratchett was chasing them, or anything with Vincent Price. So, I found the fancy slider doodahs of piano and tv cabinet fame and got 'er done. Slid them suckers all the way down a twenty-eight-foot hallway, through a kitchen piled on three and half sides with bins, and into the dining room little wee casement window area, where I figured it would look really nice behind the table

. . . also, the only place it would fit and still give off some lovely heat on a cold day . . . or even tomorrow, as noted, since this is Canada and we just wait about four hours to experience all four seasons.

It looks so nice over there . . . and now I need to unpack the rest of this damn room so I can get at it.

# CHAPTER 71

Today was Plumberdude Day! And what a day it was. They arrived, right on schedule (who knew??) and right away began. They turned on the sumptuous pump and it ran for over three straight hours . . . I think I'm glad they were here. You should've heard the car.

A company that shows up when they say, does what they say they'll do, and gets it all done, and it comes in at the quoted price—doesn't get any better. The work is done, everything is drying out and all working well. I have a sweet new water outlet outside, along with my very own really cute waterfall into the ditch. Not everybody gets one of those, you know. EJ Mac Plumbing, out of Peterborough, awesome.

While all this delightful tsunami redirection was going on outside, I had my own epic relocation therapy happening on the inside. More bins, boxes, and bags of stuff and things. I thought I had gotten rid of a lot before. I was wrong. Incorrect, mistaken, and erroneous. I did find a few treasures, however. Books. I love books, I don't know about you, but I love them. I always have. Ten years old, flashlight under the covers, reading the latest Nancy Drew I just got for my birthday at 1:45 am on a school night . . . they'll never know. They knew. Mom would ask me how the book was, did I enjoy it or did I read it so fast, I didn't know? Ha ha. Nancy, Bess, and the gang have their own box; I haven't seen it yet. Maybe they're out there solving the mysteries of the shed. Somehow, I doubt it. The Agatha Christies came later. Same deal with the flashlight, only this time, it was later since I was older. Cherished books and great memories. I have them. All of them. Every. Single. One.

Some of the kids' things, too. Games, puzzles, fun family memories. I sent the kids a few pictures . . . much laughter over the interwebs this afternoon about the fun things they did when they were younger. We did as a family. All those things. Good, strong memories for right now, especially during these times of trouble.

Sending hugs to all of you. Hold your heart strong and may your love for each other be a beacon to see you home. Of course, if you're having a vodka and soda when you get there, all the better! Cheers!

# CHAPTER 72

Another good news kind of day. I got some cookbook stuff done this morning and then I took the afternoon off! Woohoo!!

I Went Golfing!! Yahoo! My good buds E and B messaged the other day that they had booked a tee time this afternoon, would I like to join them?? Hell Ya! Especially if I can find my golf clubs. I know they're here somewhere . . . Ah . . . there they are, beside the fridge. Isn't everybody's?

Ok, shoes . . . hmmmm . . . Not enough black swoopy golf shoes, maybe there's another pair of something. Yes, some new ones I got this past season, lovely. Now . . . balls tees, hmm. I think they're here in a Ziploc somewhere. Beside the other fridge?? In the piano bench? In the Shed?? God have mercy. I finally find them in the hat and mitt bench in the back hall. Don't ask, I can't tell ya.

So now I have all the things and OMG . . . I get to go out somewhere and do something with SOMEONE ELSE! I'm not worried about distancing or all the protocols, it's fine, I'm happy to do that. As noted in a prior missive, I've been distanced from my golf ball for years. Now I just have to distance from everything and everyone else, too. No big deal. So, I excitedly run around, because, as was also noted the other day, it's the ONLY way to run, to gather up the stuff and get ready to go.

I suddenly realize the fact that I AM going out . . . omg . . . where's the lipstick? Holy crap, I haven't had that on since March 13. Where the heck . . . oh wait, phew . . . there it is, my god, where it belongs, on a shelf. Who knew something in my house could be where it belonged? Boggles the mind. So now I'm ready . . . Nope. I look in the mirror, what the hey, go full out. Earrings. Where in the H-E-double-hockey-sticks can they be? Oh, in the drawer with the other stuff. Ok, first matching pair goes in. Oh, good. Nothing matches. Wait, ok, there's a small pair, perfect. Now, if I can only find my ears, oh there they are just hiding under twenty-two pounds of hair.

Annnnd there's no holes left. It's been so long; they've disappeared like concerts, wearing button pants, and shopping without a mask. I'll huff and I'll puff and OUCH! Ok, there's one. Without further ado (I do not know what ADO means but everyone says it), I quickly I finish that chore and make my way out the door. Oh wow . . . reality . . . real human things, I can't believe it. And it was the BEST!

Seeing girlfriends, teeing up and no issue with distance . . . never came close to distance. Didn't need to worry . . . I was tripping over the thing every shot. The others had a great day, too. Wiping hair out of the way for the millionth time, I said to E, who is one of those being nominated for sainthood as a hairdresser, that I would gladly pay her for an online tutorial on how to cut my own hair. The hard part of the day was remembering not to help out with clubs, handing balls, then the non-handshake and virtual hug at the end. If we all do our part, hopefully it will help. The golf ball sure bought into the whole thing. So did the pain med I took before I left . . . still at a distance from my aches and pains going away any time soon. Hopefully, tomorrow. As the Shed groans . . . sorry, buddy, MY pain meds. I know you're a whole lot older than me, but suck it up, buttercup. Next time you move cabinets, pianos, fireplaces, then golf, we'll talk!

# CHAPTER 73

Sit back, relax, take the day . . . Oh, wait . . . another Pinky and The Brain weekend coming up! Or Ground Hog Day, take your pick.

I had ordered a few goodies from my friend, Cathy Oliffe-Webster, a.k.a. Cold Lake Cathy, cuz I saw them and I just wanted them! You know how that is, right? Especially now when we're all spending so much time at home and too much time looking at what we don't have. Well, none of you possibly as much as me, but so be it. I loved these things when I saw them on her page and just had to have them. A couple of lovely cards and a beautiful mug! I just love it! Thank you so much, Cathy, for sending so promptly so I get to enjoy them sooner!

Also, more neighbourly love today.

I heard some strange noises out the side of the house this afternoon while I was working away. You know how you try to catalogue the sounds??

Nope, that's not the sump pump . . . no, the water pump . . . wait a second, is that Newman? Scrabbling sounds? Agghhh, NEWMAN!!! Oh, thank god. Not Newman. But strange noises, just the same. My lovely next door neighbour F was cutting down the tree behind the propane tanks. What a sweetie. Thank you so much. Such good neighbours and friends they've been to me. I'm going to miss them . . . they are moving . . . sniff. But they still have family here so they'll be around. They can't get away that easily!

On to happy hour online with the girls, another virtual visit with an old neighbour and a new friend, on to online Camp Everywhere Trivia, then time to crash.

I think of the kindnesses I experienced today. We can show each other. Not difficult to do, not hard to fathom. Be kind and kindness will come back to you. Pretty simple concept.

Be kind, everybody.

# CHAPTER 74

There was such a great reception for some of the recipes I've shared, with folks enjoying reading them, some even trying them out, that I thought I'd share a few more. There may be some good Sunday cooking here. Since today was a hailstorm, rainstorm, sunshine, hot/cold kind of day, food was all I could think about and everything I tried to avoid! Seems fitting to share some "how to cooks" with you.

Some of the recipes are really perfect for this time we are going through. Page 75. I especially liked the "Invalid Drink."

"Pour juice of lemon over egg. Allow to stand 5 minutes. Beat, and add juice of orange."

It doesn't say if we're supposed to then drink it, put it in the icebox (this is 1953, after all) or pour it on the invalid, thereby invoking an instant cure. I am none the wiser. It is Sunday, however, so I suggest running outside and looking up. Watch for geese. It does seem rather fitting that it follows two punches and a lemon syrup. After getting punched several times, possibly an invalid drink is required. Maybe we could all use a dose of that right now, even if we think there's nothing wrong.

The next group that made me chuckle was page 74. I read most books like this from back to front, don't you?

Peach Conserve, Peach Marmalade, Peach Jam, Marmalade (no peach), then followed by Bath Salts. I wondered if, after all that peach, you required a bath. Nary a peach in sight on that one. Peached Out in 1953.

I am always so impressed by the no-nonsense recipes of the past. Simple, straight forward ingredients and directions. So easy to follow.

Maybe tomorrow I'll get punched, peached, jammed, conserved, then become an Invalid. It's probably the only thing you can safely do at a distance . . . no one else will want to share your pain.

# CHAPTER 75

So #75 . . . probably #76, since I think I had a mis-numbering malfunction earlier.

A few things to share with everyone!

I thought if I'm sharing recipes, I decided I had better try one myself. Others have and reported they are delicious! Of course, except the invalid one . . . they might still be invalids . . . just more . . .

So, ladies and gentlemen, I present Banana Bread, courtesy of page 7 and Helen Kennedy . . . nice catch on the Kennedy. I would love to find out if Helen is connected to this dwelling of epic proportions in which I currently reside. Maybe the shed would know. The lovely man who cuts my grass knew a little. I dropped some bread there as I delivered grass cutting funds. I was telling him, from over there, about the old cookbook, the house, and so forth and he told me of Tweedie Bay, which was the name before the present one of Kennedy. I know from a bit of research into the past that the Tweedies owned a considerable farm which fronted on the water somewhere here in our basin. I would think the Kennedys may have come later with more land. Hopefully, I'll get to find out. He is looking for photos and info.

I also got to more unpacking!! Omg, who knew it could happen.

Salt and Peppers R Me. A few to get on with, as Nana would say. More than a few, Nan. Four hundred and thiry-fire pair or thereabouts. Here's just a couple . . .

Pair #2. Toof Paste & Brush—always fun when you're five and playing dentist.

Pair #330 toaster and #425 coffee & tea, #404 to show the spoon ran away with the tea pot and not the dish, as previously reported to children everywhere.

These gave precious hours of fun for an only child in an adult world.

And, just for laughs . . . Pair #146: a pair of raccoons I've named the Newmans! Seriously, I thought I'd die laughing when I found those.

The other fun thing I found was an old show program from a production of *Guys and Dolls* from high school in 1978. Oh my. Right up there with old recipes. Too much fun.

I think. I hesitate uttering the "O" word but it's hovering when I see my childhood and teenage years flash by with every box I open. Oh well, it happens to all of us, if we're lucky!

# CHAPTER 76

Sharing all of this with all of you is helping me get me through this wild time we're all in and hopefully some chuckles and head shakes at my daily mishaps.

Today, we have unpacking of epic proportions and some shaker news too.

I unpacked a treasure trove of childhood today. So many memories in two boxes; I had a few tears. Many of these, as I noted the other day, I played with as a small child. Some I wasn't allowed to touch and others weren't interesting to a toddler. But now, they're all here and spread out on my couch in all their radiant glory!

Picture this!

A tableau of wildlife . . . all centred around a dog who found his hydrant . . . a pair of dachshunds and a few laughing crocodiles!

The next one is transportation. I loved this set of salt and peppers. A car with accompanying gas pumps. Many an hour I spent playing dinky cars with those, for a little girl who didn't have any dinky toys or brothers with dinky toys, it was awesome! I would be allowed to pick out several different sets each visit, play with them but I had to put them back if I wanted other ones. Only so many per visit. Missy Olive was very good to me and Harry, who always smelled of White Owl cigars and books from Britnell, where he worked for about fifty years, would look on with indulgence as the wee girl from next door visited again.

For those who were asking for recipes, I have another one for you. I spoke with my friend, Shirley M, today who tells me that Lazy Daisy Cake is the absolute best! It was repeated in her 1967 centennial edition of the same cookbook so it was definitely a keeper. Enjoy!!

# CHAPTER 77

Good Morning! Coffee's calling.

Today was a mixed bag. Kind of like the salt & peppers. I thought I'd share a quick bit of background.

I have salt & pepper shakers from every time zone. They are from all over the world and from many decades of the 1900's. Several are really unique, some are definitely P Incorrect and some are just plain fun. They are not fun, however, when they are in boxes, wrapped in paper and so small you are afraid you leave half of them behind every time you unwrap a set. During the life of these little guys, war, depression, talking pictures, television, computers have all made an appearance. So many events unfolded over the past ninety to a hundred years that these little collectables have seen it all. Not bad, for a bunch of little figurines. Now, it's time for them to make an appearance in my house. I hope they like it here.

I found a few other gems that surfaced through the Ocean of Bins here. The 1960's called, they want their stuff back! Oh my god, the vintage butter dish. It was on our counter and table growing up and beyond. Mom didn't see any need to change it since it wasn't broken! It was right up there with the multi-flowered, two directional wallpaper that seemed to adorn every second wall in our house. The green things that are Expo 67 souvenirs, kinda funky. At least they're not harvest gold! A little Mickey & Minnie, too. A coffee pot? That was for Sunday and for company; most often, both occurred on the same day. Probably still makes excellent coffee. It was a rare treat instead of the instant Nescafé. Feeling a bit like the rest of the planet, myself, as I tentatively open up all this stuff and take baby steps into this new world.

Also, briefly, for those folks who have been enjoying the recipes I'll share one of my grandmother's. Hope you like it!

# CHAPTER 78

Hey there. G'day! Hope your coffee is hot and you are not! I think the rain cooled us all off. Hope there was no damage where you're at. A whole lotta shakin' goin' on last night for sure. The Lake was on the take!

It was a busy one. Lots to see and be seen to. As my dad used to say while looking out the window, "I'm going to survey the master estate." Translation: go outside to the garage and see if the weed wacker will start, come back with beer. My mom would look out the window at our in-town lot with suburban house on it, take another drag on her cigarette and say, "Uh huh . . . how about taking the garbage out with you, while you're surveying." The neighbourhood kids called my dad "Mr. Fixit" and he could usually fix most things with a dinner knife and some WD40. I looked out my own window over the last couple of days and saw paint, the leaning tower of clothesline Polesa going on in the backyard, some ancient air conditioner removals, plus various items of inside excitement. The list does go on. The curse of an older estate definitely not located in suburbia, for which I count my blessings. I was introduced to a fellow and his wife yesterday who do maintenance work on master estates and I was thrilled. So now, I'm going to have some Mr. and Mrs. Fixit happening here at the Bay.

Fabulous!! There is, as you may be aware if you are tuning in here and there to my tome of timely adventure, no small pile of "fix its" to be dealt with here. I'm thinking these folks can help. I'm Mrs. "I think I can fix it" but definitely not absolutely Fix It because I might not know how. I wonder if they can find the spoons? So off I flew to town today to purchase clothesline accoutrements, some new door handles and fabric softener. Well, you need that if you are going to hang your clothes on the line, right? Bounce sheets aren't going to work, silly. Had a socially distant bevie with good friends, B & B, before heading back.

Meanwhile, Mr. & Mrs. F'it had measured and looked and scanned and measured some more. Wonderful! The master estate is getting some love. Except now, with all this rain, blowing winds and nonsense out there right now, I have some of Mother Nature's teardrops wanting to visit inside the front porch through the old windows. S I G H. All might have to wait in lieu (not LOU) of a caulking gun and sealer. Or maybe new windows . . .

hopefully, the rags piled in each window sill dry by morning then I'll see how bad it is . . .

# CHAPTER 79

It is Socially Distant Gathering in Groups of 10 Day here. What's happening where you are?

It was a busy one at the old homestead today. In addition to processing that new news on the radio this morning, I was finding, putting, placing, and getting gone some stuff!

It is always a good feeling when stuff can get gone when you want it to! Much better than not knowing where the heck it is in the first place. I had several pieces of furniture that just don't fit anymore after they finally came home. Sounds a bit like moving back home after college. You never quite fit again and they always want you in bed by ten. After copious adjustments of space and place, my desk table and the tea trolley of yore went down the road. A neighbour was very happy to receive them. I had been so excited to use the table as my desk and went through great contortions to get it in there but it doesn't work. The trolley was a find twenty years ago, which still didn't have the right location. So all is good in the furniture hood. Where all is not good is the porch. The leakage was seepage in the window sills and I'm thinking a priority shift is required. Caulking, sealing, painting before anything else. Double sigh. An updated list for Mr. & Mrs. F'it. I'm starting to feel like I'm Mrs. F'it. I look like Mrs. D's Bin Factory here, with a side of OMG, where am I gonna put that and &*(*&^% it used to be here last time I looked. All the recipes we're sharing here and I haven't found one yet that uses all these ingredients and produces a wonderful finished product! I wonder if there's one for dropped calls, video messages, or texts? All that new internet folderol and things still drop with annoying regularity. The Shed is snickering again and the bunkie just continues way over there, by itself, in blissful ignorance. "Be the bunkie"—I need a new tee shirt.

In better news, how is the social distance going out there? As noted, we can now gather in groups of ten—anybody Tenning? Or have plans to? I know some of my girl buds are talking about a distance paint party for Snow and her dudes. The crew is getting a little worn. I find that hard to understand considering they just stand around all day doing nothing and refuse to help with anything. My friend, MA, heard they were getting together in groups of six but one wasn't Happy . . .

Thanks to those who have been trying some of the recipes and for reporting back. Cuz C made Nana's cookies and pronounced them delish! Nana would be very happy the clan is enjoying! Many tried the Lazy Daisy with great results. In checking through the recipes, I found Chicken Haddie Casserole, again, ca. 1953. I've never heard of chicken haddie. East Coasters? I did some research. I think it sounds interesting.

**Definition:**

"**Chicken Haddie** is a fan favourite. **Chicken Haddie** is a boneless mixture of quality white fish including cod, hake and pollock. Try it right out of the can as a tasty snack or it can be used in any recipe that requires fish such as chowders, fish cakes, or pasta."

Now the catch is, ha ha, as far as I can tell, the nearest place to get it is the Gimli Market in Manitoba. And . . . why are they calling it chicken? It's clearly fish. I'm so confused. It happens easily, be gentle. Sometimes, I just wanna Be the Bunkie.

# CHAPTER 80

A morning coffee milestone! Cup up and carry on! I can't believe I've shared my tales of angst and woe eighty times with you. My goodness, thank you for tuning in!

Today was unpacking (what else is new?) and putting away, also not new. What was new was a funny discovery that never dawned on me before today. In relocating some prized possessions to elsewhere (i.e., festive decor to the attic), daughter #2 who is doing the long-distance hauling, says from above, "You know, this and this and this and this are Christmas bins." I holler yes, rather warily, glad of the two-meter distance rule. When your children are helping, it's always nice to agree. She says, "You know, you wouldn't allow raccoons and squirrels to live up here but you've let an entire season worth of stuff sign a lease forever." Thought I'd die . . .

As I was recovering from that much needed guffaw, I was on the main floor finding out what was in a box marked "Misc." Always an adventure. When I moved the box and another bag of strangely shaped items wrapped in newspaper, I bumped a blind hanging, oddly enough, on the wall. I'd never given it much thought before, it was just part of the atmosphere.

There had always been something in front of it so I had never really paid much attention. I decide, with investigative flare, to pull it up. Well, darned if there wasn't window hiding back there. A full, very old, complete window, painted shut. I clamber over and look through the window and I see the back side of paneling. I go through the door, into the porch to look and on the other side of the paneling is hanging the saw blade . . . right over the window. Then I look closer. The blade is fastened right in the middle of the window beam since the single sheet of panel would never have supported that weight this long. I guess they really didn't want to see out that window ever again. I shake my head. How are we gonna fix this, I mutter out loud to myself. Or should we? A second huge guffaw all around. Visions of my vision of applying planking to the porch walls fizzling as I think of the fixes before the fact. I think the bad misbehaved porch just got an upgrade to permanently grounded. This porch is never going to stay out late on a Friday ever again.

The shed is chortling, the dudes are standing around doing nothing, as usual, and then there's the bunkie. The Bunkie. In distant majestic silence back there, oblivious to all the chaos around it, connected but quietly, stoically, exuding peace and tranquility. Be the Bunkie.

I'm not sure therapy will help.


# CHAPTER 81


I'm all for coffee and sitting in a soft chair, you?

A busy day here, once again, Pinky and The Brain would be proud. Same thing I do every day, unpack. A friend commented yesterday that he figured I'd be dead before I got it all unpacked. I'm starting to agree. I thought it was on the menu today. More luggery and sluggery had by all and things are really coming along. Clotheslines and air conditioning day, here. A really bad country song in the making. The handiest of dudes came today to do these remove and replace jobs and it went well. Of course, nothing goes completely as planned . . .

I had to go digging in the shed for the rest of the window piece to fit in once the old air conditioner was gone. I found it and while I was yanking it out, I could smell the mixed aroma of old lifejackets, gas, wood, and garden tools. It reminds of me the cottage when I was a kid. I love that little shed. Gives all the feels without the trouble its bigger brother does. The other thing I found was a wasp nest, right in the eaves above the window pieces. Agh. They were not impressed. That made two of us. I did, however, learn something new today. A spritz of WD40 after dark, that universal fix-it device, would settle the situation once and for all. I did not know that. I didn't have any so nothing got settled, but it is good to know.

Moving along to the clothesline; that was another fun-filled and exciting event. How could it be anything else? The old one was strung through the trees and on the wonky pole beside the oblivious bunkie. A huge, tall black iron pole, stretching into the trees and leaning like the big bad wolf would only need half a puff to blow it down. The shiny new clothesline was fun. A stake in the ground, fastener, and voilà! Except, not voilà. It's never voilà the first time, this is me . . . you know that. The voilà never happened and still isn't happening. They dug several "test holes" to find out the best location. Apparently, there is more rock down there than Flintstone and Rubble have ever seen and not enough depth to plant the thing. Much digging, moving, shoving, and finally a spot was found. Some wobble. A metal shim was needed and we didn't have any. Nothing in the magic shed except wasps. I began canvassing the neighbourhood. The super grass guy had some and the neighbour down the street had some, too. I walked back with one while the golf cart appeared with the other. Awesome place, by the Bay. Everybody helping out.

Even more helping out was going on inside. Daughter strikes again with lug and slug. The kid deserves a medal. I'll give her one from the traction ward while I recover from the ache and pain of every muscle and bone I possess. Thank god the light at the end of the tunnel is slightly visible now and not hiding in the form of some other massive piece of household goods that needs to be somewhere else. The day ended with the first campfire of the season and finally, a hug! The best gift of all ♥.

# CHAPTER 82

Coffee with cream, so supreme! Well, sugar-free creamer but nonetheless . . . or more . . . as the case may be. As you can tell, I'm off to the races with my day off report.

The day off was awesome. I have found that sometimes you just gotta. I thought I would update you on a few finds within the confines of the box and binlands. A few foibles of functionality that came to light during my forage through far flung fangled fiascos. Say that fast about six times . . .

First up, a really neat little what's-it that was my mom's. This little doo-hickey used to sit somewhere in the kitchen, close to the stove so it makes me think it was for spoons or other weaponry of kitchen creation used for cooking. Cute in a late 1950's kind of way. The lid comes off, which makes me think of something losing its head in the nonsense that surrounds me.

The second discovery was an S&P set of two little kitties. Reminds me of Cold Lake Cathy and her cat tales, mugs, and cards. Thought of you, Cathy, as soon as I opened the box and they were peering up at me with that look of disdain cats are so famous for. Love them! Into the cabinet with the rest of the 522 pair. Well, only 61 at this point. The big Shed is hogging the boxes of the rest. No fessing them up just yet, ya rotten scoundrel! Wait 'til I sic the Bunkie on you . . . Bunkie says, "Uh, uh . . . no way. Peace man . . ."

The third thing was kind of an "OMG, I forgot about this" find. My original family name was Haarsma. A long story worth about forty-five chapters. Suffice it to say, the name was changed . . . in about 1948 or so with no explanation or information to my dad or his siblings. This is your new name, no longer use your old one. Make of that, what you will. None of them ever said and the rest of us live on in wonder and confusion. Any family out there with insight? So fast forward to June 0, 1984, or back, as the case may be. My dad was Production Manager at Goodwill, in charge of donations received at the main facility in Toronto. He received this letter in the mail regarding their clothing department. I believe they had a number of areas where items were manufactured for sale to help fund the works of Goodwill Industries. I would imagine that is what this letter refers to. The name of the company was our former family name, fairly common in Holland, not nearly so much in Canada. I'm not certain if the family ventured into import/export but the original Haarsma migrated from Holland in 1850 to New York then Pennsylvania then by Red River cart to the area that would become Winnipeg. Afterward, becoming a market gardener of some repute, with a street being named after the family and large land holdings. The farmlands were eventually sold off once the city had displaced the farms, to become part of the city of Winnipeg.

Certain branches of the family were well off; however, my great-grandfather was married twice, for a total of about eighteen children. They must've run out of names, since, like my grandfather, at least two of them were named James. He was second or third last of the second bunch, born in 1910 and eventually settling in Toronto after a myriad of locations in Manitoba and southern Ontario. For Dad to receive this letter in the mail must've caused some sort of startled reaction. I don't remember hearing of it; however, I was long gone from home at the time so I might not have. The other funny piece of the puzzle was that my Aunt Shirley was married to a man named Dunn, probably around that time and was a border broker, dealing in import/export issues daily. So many connections, so little information. I may do some research into Haarsma Import/Export and see if some of the 'Peg branch of the family ever ventured to Alberta and became import/export folks. Not right now because this story is long enough!!!

Good day, eh. Stay safe.

# CHAPTER 83

A busy one around here. First up, feeling fresher after a day off. The Shed awaits! THE Shed . . . that cute, little, unassuming bundle of dubious integrity and joy. Smirking, as I struggle with the lock and flip the hasp. The door opens on a cornucopia of creepy cardboard, second only to the wee privy which is only privy to crap, as far as I can tell. The Shed is being searched this fine day, for items of dump-worthy proportion. Lovely neighbours are doing a run and suggested if I had anything, it was welcome to go along. Well, I just might need my own access to a trucking company to fulfill that task. I might know a guy . . .

The Shed grumbled and groused, argued and in a not-so-polite fashion, fessed up a veritable pile of interesting stuff. Some albums from high school and beyond . . . John Denver being my all-time favourite musician and so many memories from all this vinyl. Judy Garland, a feast of 45s. Dance lesson 45s . . . ?? Who does that? I can see dance lesson 78s . . . 33s . . . But 45s? Any 45s I had are rock 'n roll or "Silhouettes on the Shade," my all-time favourite song. Dance lessons?? My Gawd. I can already dance, I hope. I'll have to scare up a turntable somewhere . . . maybe there's one in here in Nana Shepherd's old 1948 hi fi.

VHS tapes of my mom's. Scottish fiddle music and Jurassic Park . . . I'm not sure what that's trying to say. I have visions of dinosaurs doing the Gay Gordon. Just try to unsee that. The dinosaurs are in with Presumed Innocent so I guess they maybe didn't dance after all. After seeing this, I may never dance again, either. A pile of Miche purse covers . . . oh my. Into the donate box they go. Haven't used one of those in a long, long time. Clothes that no longer need me. More donations. Some spoons . . . my goodness gracious, could it be possible. No. These spoons are big guys. Silver and the baby spoons our kids used that we all hang onto for grandkids or guest kids who need to eat. And two keepsakes. Things didn't change much between older and younger daughter at school doing handprints. Same sweet poem, four years apart. Touched my heart, finding these.

I managed to get them out of the clutches of the abyss and out into the yard and the deck. There were many things hitting the dump pile: an old coffee maker, holy seat cushion probably only needed on Sundays, cords, boxes, and assorted flotsam and jetsam of nonsense better gone than present. So, there will be a pile for the dump run and pile for donations. At least the pile that can be used is free and the unusable one might cost some coin. Worth it in the end to be rid of the junk. But you should hear the Shed. I was surprised the handy dude guy who finished the clothesline didn't hear it groaning and carrying on over there. Maybe he did . . . he wasn't here long . . .

Sigh. Be the Bunkie.

Stay tuned tomorrow when I tell you about the letter from 1949.

# CHAPTER 84

I was going to relate a tale of a letter today, however, events today have pre-empted that story. Film at 11.

About a three weeks ago, when I was thinking of doing more things with this den of iniquity in which I live, I called the Habitat for Humanity Restore and asked about cabinetry. They often get donations of kitchen cabinets and said they didn't have any but would be happy to put me on the list and call me if some came in. I was in town this morning dropping off something to my girlfriend, EH. We had a lovely distant coffee and enjoyed catching up. While I was leaving, I got a call from the Restore. They had one, did I want it? Oh boy. I had had folks in for information on some updates and was awaiting results. Since I was only five minutes from the place, I went to look. Well, it had most of the parts needed and what configurations aren't there, could be gotten. I called my rehab guy and he said he could make it happen. So, off to the races. But you know how I said I had done my last U-Haul? I lied. After I decided this could work, off I went to rent a truck and load it up. The cabinetry was loaded, the truck in gear and away we go! Arriving home with my exciting find, daughter #2 and neighbour, F, helped unload. Now I have a plethora of oak in my living room awaiting design and install.

I'm thinking it will be great, like most things, when it's done. I'm hoping the doing is as much fun as the end. As we ran through the briars and the brambles lugging the heavy large shapes and sizes, the seven dudes stood in awe as we shuffled our humps back and forth. Not lifting one finger to help, they radiated silent disdain. Thank god the Shed didn't mess this one up. It was probably glad to have me focus on something else so it was out of the spotlight and could quietly plot with the dudes when nobody was looking.

# CHAPTER 85

Hey there all, you crazy folks out there. You must be, you're tuning into this ongoing saga of situations sometimes to see what the latest is to befall yours truly.

I did promise the story of the letter from 1949.

Briefly (haha) it is from my grandfather to his sister in Scotland about the rental of a summer cottage for several weeks in the summer of 1949 on Rice Lake, just outside Peterborough. My mother was fourteen at the time, her sisters four and six years older, respectively. Out in the work world, they join the family for a weekend at the lake. Fishing, boating, and resting were the highlights of the vacation, much treasured by city dwellers who loved to embrace all aspects of their adopted country they now called home. Originally from Aberdeen and Glasgow, my grandparents met in Toronto after each had arrived separately from the old country. My grandfather speaks of neighbours and friends visiting, all of whom I have vague recollections of as folks who came in and out of our lives, and Hogmanay celebrations like visitors to the Centre Island fun park. Always there, not for long, but just as much fun as the last time. And always, the Scottish lilt in the background of voices and laughter at practical jokes, events, and memories of happenings at home. The Scottish, while known for their thrift, have a wicked sense of humour and such, poking fun at each other was a frequent pastime that always made me, the oldest grandchild on that side, watch and listen with wonder and awe. Shy and timid, I learned a great deal about fun and laughter in a kind way and teasing because you love someone, not because you mean to be hurtful. Invaluable lessons to a little girl.

My grandfather never, ever went back to Scotland after he arrived in Canada. He missed the family dreadfully, but I think he worked hard for a roof over their heads and food on the table and did not spare the money for a trip back. My grandmother missed it terribly, so finally, before my mother was born in 1935, my grandmother and the two girls were sent over to visit and ended up staying two months while he saved for the passage to bring them back.

I was gifted this letter by my cousin, Kate, when I was over for a visit. I can't remember the details of how she ended up with it but I was very grateful to have it as it told the story of my family in a brief time when they took time to enjoy their new country and their family in cottage country. I think there is a genetic component to enjoying the lake. And then going on to write about it 😊.

Speaking of writing about it, it is fitting that I share this now. A number of you have suggested that these musings should be a book. I want to take this time to tell you that I've taken that step and the first thirty chapters plus photos are at the publisher now, to be titled *If This House Could Talk*. I am not certain of the publish date; however, I guess it depends how quickly we get through the editing process. I want to thank all of you so much for the support! Book is in the works, as well, so hopefully #1 flies off the shelves like Newman's escape. Maybe the Bunkie will talk to the Shed and between them, the dudes, and the car, they'll can all get along long enough to tell all their friends!

# CHAPTER 86

Today's adventures were not nearly as exciting as the previous one. You might remember the tv tower with the tree and the Christmas lights dangling for all and sundry, most likely for many years. When I bought this place, there were lights all around. A lovely idea; the folks prior to me loved the season and decorated accordingly. Sadly, over time, the lights fell into disrepair and straggled from various locations around the house. I had tried to resuscitate them but it was beyond even this lifeguard.

Today, since my lovely neighbours, J & F, are leaving me next week for other locales, we decided to do the "retrieve the lights from the tower" trick before they go. F was kind enough earlier this month to trim and cut the trees, which had taken up residence in the old tower and since the tower was now visible and available for use as a ladder, the game was afoot. Well, my foot was game, let's put it that way. I clambered up, up, up . . . I felt like the Friendly Giant. Look waaay up! Definitely room at the bottom for two more to curl up in . . . especially if they land head first or on their arse, they'll be curled up just fine.

Memories flooded back of climbing up the tower as a kid to get onto the second-floor roof to put lights on the overhang at the front of the house. Two full floors, rather than the paltry storey and half today. However, I was twelve years old the time. At sixty, it's a different kettle of fish. These fish would've been fried if I'd done a header. So I go gingerly at first, since the trip is intertwined with tree limbs and stray light cords. Sunlight is blasting over the height of the roof directly into my eyes. From down below, "Watch the branch . . . careful of the twig, make sure you've a good hold." All very caring and kind, as I'm wrapped up with both arms around each level and not sure of where to put my feet next. Slowly, I ascend each level, making sure my big feet get solidly on the crossbar before I grab overhead. Finally, I'm there. Then, as I'm grabbing the lights and pulling, the string gets stuck on the top rung by one dinky light. I'm not on the top rung. I'm reaching, from three rungs below. Reach for The Top comes to mind in a half-baked memory . . . omg . . . not now, no laughs right now. Meanwhile, from the ground, there's a camera snapping pictures interspersed with "Don't JUMP." Great neighbours . . . LOL. Then, as I finally the get the lights free, I drop them to the ground. OMG . . . that is another thing off the copious list. I can just hear the rest of the neighbourhood as they drive past the little driveway: "Oh, where did those lights go?? Didn't there used to be lights hanging down??" "I wonder if the deer chewed them . . . maybe the bears got them." "Bears???" "Omg I didn't know we had bears . . . lock the car door, Ethel."

See, this is how rumours start. All because I got sick of looking at half a string of dangling red Christmas lights ca. 1968. Happy New Year.

# CHAPTER 87

I'm not sure what it's like where you are but it's pretty warm here these days. Lovely and hot, summer is here; it might finally be safe now to take the snow brush out of the car. We're probably good to get those snow tires off, as well. Just saying . . . it is not my fault if it snows next week.

Today's adventures were enough to warm up your cup with. I had gotten the air conditioner that came from British Columbia. It was finally warm enough to try it out. It is installed beautifully and ready to go, as soon as I figure out how to turn it on without blowing it up. It has a remote . . . doesn't everything these days? I would like a remote for my life. I wonder if it would work after the first try?? As I was saying, I first had to figure it all out. As I read the directions, since I am a female, I do that (I can't wait to hear it) and discover that I need to set it one step at a time or things don't work. I figure out the sequence from page get all revved up to go, and then discover the plug on it requires the space of about three GFI receptacles, very long with extra doodads on it. I look at my outlet, confusion and concern brewing better than my 1957 percolator. Because the outlet is set into the brickwork behind the propane stove, the plug won't fit in it. Nothing I try will make this fit. Sigh. Take out a brick? Can you just imagine what that might cause? It does not bear thinking about. I guess I need an extension cord, thinks I, out loud. What good are all these revelations of rectitude if you keep them to yourself? The plug itself could contact Tokyo and order dinner at the same time, it is that huge. Set and test, the buttons say. There could be complications. I find a cord that might work and I plug it in, expecting "voilà" or something equally exciting, to appear on the screen. Instead, I get Mode/Reset/Temp all flashing in beautiful synchronicity with me no further ahead. Page 3, coming up. I finally figure out the sequence, hit the magical "On" button, and my god, it works! I'm feeling pretty good about things, about thirty minutes in. The house is cooling down, things are going according to plan. I go down to the back fridge where all manner of utilities are located and happen to glance, in passing, at the frowning power bar which currently runs the water pump. No light on the power bar. So the water pump is off. I start thinking about it . . . the A/C is sucking all the power. They are on the same line. Jeez $&@%# etc. I turn the thing off and check the water pump—the light is back on. I begin looking to see the next closest outlet. It's over there. Way longer away than my cord. I think I am destined to overheat. Just like the cord that is feeling warm as I disconnect it from the A/C unit. I can't win. I'm glad the plumber dude is coming soon to deal with the pumps. Hope he brings enough cords or really big power bars or maybe a power dude. I think it's going to be that kind of summer. Keep cool and don't trip on your cords.

# CHAPTER 88

A different type of day here. I actually even left town. You will never believe this but things actually went according to plan! Oh my freakin gawd! Who knew it could happen?? Nobody tell the shed.

I had a meeting with a couple handy type dudes about some work on the house. This, between assembling more stuff for the dump and cleaning up the yard. I couldn't believe it. Got the canoe racked, stuff organized, and half a plan for this upcoming work. Holy Great Mother of Pearl . . . could something be trying to go in the right direction? I had then planned a visit to my daughter. I have not seen her face to face since October so this was huge! I also had not seen her new place so it was very huge, indeed. We have all been struggling these past months with not being able to see family so I was very excited we were finally able make it happen. She had prepared a lovely meal, and we shared a wonderful chat and catch up. Felt so good for this mama. Mrs. Fixit, here, helped out a bit too. Marie was telling me the story of the building manager not repairing the door screens on the sliders. Apparently, a disgruntled discussion had ensued with the screens still broken. I looked at them and said, "I can fix those. Grab me a butter knife and nail polish." After Marie looked at me in shocked surprise, she fetched the items and I got to work. The screens were hanging off the frame, rubber edging askew and looked fragile. I took the knife, edge side out and pushed each section of screen back in the frame, sealing it with the rubber edging. After knifing the whole perimeter of the frame, the screen was back in place and the seal secure. This only works if the screen isn't ripped. Then I sealed all the corners with the nail polish, holding the edging in place. Repeat on door number two. I didn't think to take a picture of the "before" but the after looks super, if I do say so myself. And I do.

Happy girl, happy mom, with a bit of screening thrown in for good measure. All and all, a lovely day. ☺

# CHAPTER 89

Thanks for tuning in for the continued saga of situations. I appreciate the support. Anybody need to be screened? I'm your girl. I found out today that heat hurts. When I went for my haircut, I also grabbed a fifty-foot heavy duty power cord. That darn air conditioner was going to work if it killed me. I was afraid it might. After the glory of haircut heaven, I rushed home to try it out. I decided to plug it into the front of the house. I could've plugged it into the neighbours' house, it was long enough, but I didn't think they'd appreciate that. Insert Technical term voilà! It worked! It started cooling things down pretty quickly. I cautiously turned on a fan to help the cause and it kept working, too! My gawd, don't tell the shed.

I went outside to assess the temperature. I need to keep on keepin' on with the sheds (aaagghh) because another dump run cometh. It was way too hot to lug and slug today. Maybe tomorrow will prove better. Way too hot to cook, too! I had offered to make breakfast for my lovely neighbours who move away tomorrow. But who wants to turn on an oven? Can't do breakfast muffins on the bbq . . . so I decided I'd try the toaster oven. I did make sure to turn the A/C off first, just, you know, in case. I hear you out there. One of these handydudes needs to be an electrician or know one or at least know one that knows one or something. A toaster oven for muffins works great. Then I delivered them and yogurt next door. I had put my drink in the freezer while I did this, promptly forgetting about it when I came back and decided to jump in the lake to cool off. Lovely!!! But when I went to get ice cubes for my next straight cranberry, (I know, I know) it was a frozen solid mass of red cranberry slurpie. Everything can't go according to plan around here, it wouldn't be right. I mean, you aren't new here and neither am I. That just doesn't happen. But red cranberry slurpie could be a new thing. I began thinking how I could jazz the thing up. Vodka, of course. It might not freeze, then. Maybe the vodka could soak in. That might be an answer. Frozen Vodka Cranberry Splash. Hmmm. It might've been done already but not by me. So I take the vodka out of the freezer and add a bit. I'll be darned if the little Darlin' didn't start melting right away. Well, a cure for heat exhaustion does exist! Just make sure you have your toaster oven off first and sit in front of your air conditioner so when you fall over, you'll cool off right away.

You're welcome.

# CHAPTER 90

A bittersweet day in the Baylands today. My lovely neighbours, who I've mentioned a number of times, who catch me from great heights, helped with food and groceries throughout my Q time and are just all-around Super Neighbours, moved away today. Not far, but not next door anymore either. Sniff of huge proportions. They have been the kindest to me over my time of trouble and need and I want to thank them most humbly and with gratitude and warmth. They helped me with a place to stay, a place for my stuff when I needed it, and created a huge place in my heart. The muffins and yogurt I delivered last evening and dinner for tonight is a small offer of thanks. They invited me to join in distant breakfast this morning with them, so I did.

I thought I was breaking bread with Abbot and Costello. J tells me about something, F makes a joke, J says, "No, it's my story," F says, "What story?" J says, "Let me finish my story." F says, "Ok." J is stumped. Didn't expect a simple "ok." Thought I would choke on my pineapple with fibre. I'm going to miss them in the next door to mine but when we can, I'll visit their new door and hope I can give them a chuckle or two. Maybe I can finish a story.

After breakfast, a good friend came out to discuss kitchen rip and reno. Has he got some fan-fab ideas for the sea of cabinetry currently abiding in the living room! Can I get a woohoo? The best part?? He starts this week! Yeehaw, it's going to be busy and crazy and exciting and wild. Or just another day in the life of me. I think I need to order the bunkie shirt today.

After this fun and excitement, I golfed with a few good friends I haven't golfed with or seen since last year. It was nine holes of pure delight. You ever golfed with Curly, Larry & Moe? I was Shep . . . quiet, non-talkative . . . ok, I tried to be Shep, I tried really hard. It's hard to laugh at stories all separated by golf carts but we did! The patio has opened there so we had a distant apres-golf libation and snack. Was it ever wonderful to do something quasi normal! Laugh with those three and then wrap it all up on the patio after-wards—priceless! Followed up by the daily dunk in the lake—a super day!

It did my soul the world of good. The other thing doing my soul good is the recipes I'm finding for yum stuff! The recipe for peach schnapps slushy looks delicious.

# CHAPTER 91

You could have a day just like mine . . . wait a minute, "No, no, no" I heard you yelling from here!

Is anybody else having phone trouble? I cannot believe how long it takes to get phone service sorted out with the mother corp. Even Mork could get through to Orson faster than this. I had a couple of calls to make this morning so I made them on my walk about the 'hood. Got to keep active, these corona calories are killing me. So I walk approximately 5500 steps on the first walk, early when it's not quite so humid. Hot today; it was 8C by 8:30 am. That's 82.4F for the metrically-challenged among us, myself included. It's only been forty years since we went metric; I'm a slow learner.

I'm chatting away, walking, any neighbours out must've figured I'd finally lost it, striding along talking to myself if they didn't see the ear bud cord. Folks waving, stopping and so forth. None of it interrupted my call. As I came back around to pass the house and head up the hill, boom. The call got fuzzy then went dead. How did it know we were passing the Shed? The car was right there, I bet it told everybody else. Even the dudes were staring in disbelief. They usually stare in solemn ignorance and bliss so disbelief was an upgrade. As I waved back at neighbours, who were waving at me, I sensed a calm coming from the Bunkie as I went past. Ahhhh. Peace. Well, the Bunkie doesn't make phone calls . . . maybe it does, in the dead of night, maybe it knows a guy who knows a guy. Maybe that's why there was disbelief for the dudes. Then I had to hit redial and start the whole bit of nonsense over again. It worked until I travelled down the road and back then promptly quit again. I got onto the direct chat to inquire WHEN I might have proper phone service restored. I got "we are looking into this for your utmost in service" or some such jabberwocky. My utmost is not serviceable for any length of time at all. I had a couple of jealousy pangs today when the biggest phone company in the country arrived next door to install a dish for the new neighbour. We shall see if this assists my persistent bad service.

In other news that would not assist telephone calls, holy tornado Batman! A whirlytwirl right across the lake this evening. It kept to the northern side and, unfortunately, did considerable damage in several places. Thankfully, no one was injured in the destruction. I didn't even know about it until I got a message from a friend asking if I was ok. A second friend said they hoped so, since they didn't want to miss the next chapter. Hahaha! So here you go!

# CHAPTER 92

This is your up-to-date, to-the-minute, hippy dippy morning info! And you thought I was going to say weather. C'mon, you know you did. Day followed by night . . . followed by day. There ya go. George Carlin ain't got nothin on me!

An exciting day here at the Bay, my goodness, such adventure, who knew?? OMG . . . we all knew. Nothing is easy around here. I'd love to make a complete phone call, get help from my posse of permanent statues, have a couple of buildings that didn't act up and a car that didn't chortle. You know, normal stuff. Is it too much to ask?

I decided I'd better keep looking after myself since nobody else should! I've met with varying degrees of success at this over the years. While walking almost 6,000 steps this morning (3 miles or 4.1 km) the phone calls were fine until I got back to the house. Again. That damn corner is death to phone calls. I left a message regarding service, discussed the pros and cons of internet phone online and decided smoke signals would be the most effective. It could work, I think. The fire ban is off; I have a fire pit. Plenty of wood. I scratch my head, thinking, Maybe I could burn the shed . . . Ya! No. Nobody knows how to read them anymore, anyway. I'd be talking to myself. I think I'm doing that already . . .

I think I'm in a dead phone zone here. So far, the new neighbours' "disk on the house" hasn't done diddly do for me so I guess she didn't get the memo.

I'm seriously thinking I need a phone shrink. I'd love to be on the line with them when it cuts off . . . Have I got another number they can reach me at? HA! Not from you guys, buddy. Should I put another quarter in the slot? What part of "Be part of the solution, not the problem" haven't you heard about?

In other unbreaking news, no further whirlytwirl updates here, thankfully nothing else happened out on the water today. This afternoon a neighbour came by with distant rhubarb cake . . . oh my goodness, it was lovely! Thanks so much, E, it was super. Handy guy R. the Painter also began the paint prep for the house exterior. It's going to be calm like the Bunkie. I told you we all need more Bunkie and less Shed in our lives. He was busy out there. I think I'll start calling the house F.O.R.D. Fix or repair daily. Fill holes, seal cracks, scrape paint. A fine old time. For him. At least it's a spectator sport for me. He said if I wanted the old shutters back up, he'd hand me the hammer. Nope, I think that would be an unwise move. Pianos moved, truckloads of furniture, towers climbed, I got it. Hammer/nails? Nope. I made good my escape and went to town, hunting dish sinks. What, you ask, is a dish sink? I asked the same thing. Kitchen update dude suggested one for the bathroom as part of a re-purpose of an antique dresser. Dishes in the bathroom. If the kitchen sink doesn't get hooked up fast enough, that's what it'll be.

# CHAPTER 93

Today's mind muse is in reference to coffee, unless something mind blowing happens between here and there and I'll switch gears. So far, coffee is on.

Trying to descale. In prepping and planning for the kitchen biz, I decided my Tass coffee maker needed retooling so I can make easy coffee without percolating too much trouble. So, it needs cleaning before I open one of the 4,025 Tass pods I have here, just waiting in breathless anticipation for the call. I locate the cleaning disk, hiding in the top part instead of on the slot where it is normally stored. I had already cleaned all the parts so I'm good to go. I think. A little suspicion on the disk depository. How and why is it there and not where it should be? I get one pod to try before I begin the big clean. Why? Because. I'm that much of an idiot that I want to see if it will work without the deep clean. So I fill it, turn it on. Presto. A technical term, look it up. Water begins flowing, however, not precisely where it should. I now have an instant counter cleaner and no coffee in the cup. Huge sighs ensue. Much swabbing of deck and cursing of me. I get it sorted out and, glutton for punishment that I am and since "No" just doesn't seem to be in my repertoire, I try again, only this time I use the cleaner disk. Lo and behold, eureka and all that, the noisy grindy grumbly thing starts up, just the way it should. No extra clean counter and lots of ancient coffee yuck landing in the cup. I wonder if I'll be able to make cappuccino . . . oh my. Not out of that, silly. The possibilities are endless. Coffee for Baileys. Coffee for Kahlua. Coffee for "early morning get the icky out of your eyes and wake up so you can share a story" coffee. In my upcoming kitchen chaos, I could put the thing beside the bed. Oh my! Just roll over, push the button, share a sip, a story and I'm good to go. Go where? Back to sleep comes to mind. There'll be so much piled in the room I won't be able to get out to go anywhere anyway. Might as well sip and shut eye. I might need more of that Baileys, though. If I open the window a little wider, could one of you just pass some through? Don't let the Shed see you, it'll want some and whine. Thank you so much.

Never mind the coffee, just send Baileys, Kahlua, whatever you've got. It just showed furiously blinking red lights and flashing "See User Manual See User Manual" at warp speed. I thought Scotty was in the midst of beaming it up and failed. Then it just blew up all over the aforementioned counter, soaked my shirt, decimated the pod, broke the pod poker, coffee everywhere and is going in the dump pile. Now I have 4,024 coffee pods with no machine. Somebody must've told the Shed. I told all of you to be quiet. This is why Mama drinks.

The Rest of the story? The PS? After I cleaned everything up, I looked online to see where I might be able to buy another machine. A drip, a perk, a press are evidently not enough ways to make coffee. Stores don't sell them anywhere anymore so now I am still stuck with all these pods. I decide to check the buy and sell and success! Somebody north of me is selling one for twenty-two bucks. I get it for twenty and start the car, have a lovely drive, come back and it works perfectly! Again, don't tell the shed or I'll be drinking hot water and it doesn't go with Baileys.

# CHAPTER 94

Hey there, hope everybody is well and feeling fine. I did manage coffee this morning, yay yay. Especially for me, you all just have to read this. I have to write it and without coffee, it ain't happening.

I think my real estate value just went up about 50k. A contract company was here today cutting down Emerald ash trees. What a shame to see those huge monoliths go down; however, my view went up considerably with the great demise of that partial forest. I have a much clearer view of the lake and the breeze today was not hampered by trees. As I watched yet another opportunity for entertainment out my front door, I wondered where anybody else might have this going on for them on a regular basis. Coupled with adventures in futility, you just can't buy this stuff. Of course, if anybody had been watching inside, they'd have refunded their tickets.

I spent the day starting the repacking of the unpacking of the kitchen of the last few months. I either need a bigger kitchen or just remove the whole thing instead of kitchen rehab. I've already shown I can exist with a coffee pod instead of a whole perk. I can use a microwave instead of stove/oven/crockpot/electric frypan/BBQ. I will literally be camping out.

I heard from a reliable source that overnight residential camping has been cancelled for this summer. I'm not quite sure where that leaves me. Do I make a phone call and turn myself in? What is the fine? I could go to jail, they serve food there, I wouldn't have to worry. It would be the getting out of jail part that could pose a problem. I don't have one of those Monopoly cards left over. I could finish packing the unpacked and repair myself to the nearest hotel which has room service from ten feet away. I could order breakfast in bed, lunch in the lanai, dinner from the dining room. It all sounds delightfully appealing. A getaway from my everyday. Of course, I'd have to skip out at am on the last night since I will have been paying all my dollars to various and sundry rip and replace experts and will have nothing left with which to foot the hotel bill, but I digress. Maybe I could pull the fire alarm, then everybody would be skipping out. They'd thank me, I know they would. Of course, I would have to go to some place that isn't local. There's a chance they might know me. If not before the caper, then certainly after. I'm thinking I might be best off making myself another vodka, going back out on the front porch, and watching more of this bitter saga of sagging bark unfold.

# CHAPTER 95

Today is a random Saturday, a prodigious sampling of lighthearted ramblings, take from it what you will. As long as you have a morning libation, we're good to go!

While I was cruising around the interwebs, I decided I could use a new t-shirt. I found some online that might be perfect. They looked comfortable yet a bit stylish. Maybe I could add my own stuff onto it. Daughter #1 said, "Robo Mom!!!" Oh My Gawd, Martha, that's what they called me when they were little tiny tykes. I guess some things are seared in the psyche. I'll get that on the back. I have a coffee cup that says "Don't Mess With Me, I'm the Mom." Fitting. On the front it goes.

I have continued to pack the unpacked and load the unloaded. I think I could now move anybody's anything anywhere in no time at all. Not to mention the entire "put away" thing, I mean seriously. Whose counting, but really? The kitchen looks like a bomb went off, the living room is already a write off as a newfangled type of storage unit for kitchens (oops, can't sit there, that's where the pantry sits when it's not out harassing Grumpy and Sneezy), and the dining room? Well, it's beginning to look more like somebody's mess hall with every freakin' passing minute. Oh, that would be my mess hall. I guess mess is the operative word. Insert huge, extended, overly dramatic sigh. It will all be just fine . . . later,

While I was on my walk this morning, I met a new neighbour who has been here almost sixty years. Telling, that number. He has stories, history, and a connection to this place. He asked me if the little shed was still there. I told him that it was. The little shed, who doesn't have much to do with the others, except to be in-between to keep the racket down and the conversation up. I wondered why the little shed . . . why not the bunkie? I mean, who doesn't like the bunkie? Then I remembered there was no bunkie in the B.M. Time (Before Me). I'm only the third owner so that's not bad in eighty years. He told me he had always liked the little shed because it always smelled like boats, motors, and gas. I laughed delightedly, telling him THAT'S why I like the little shed. It reminds me of my childhood cottage at Crystal Lake. Our porch smelled like that all the time as the boat gas was kept there along with lifejackets and assorted items of boat paraphernalia. I told him to c'mon down and have a sniff. So he did! So we strolled up the avenue 'til we were there (we might've been even better than Fred and Judy without the tuxedos). The scent, more faint, is still there, even after all these years and I don't have a boat and motor. It must be embedded in the very walls. I will be finding out more from my neighbour about the history of the Bay and I'm looking forward to that. Stay tuned!

In another random bit of ecstatic excitement, I went to town to grab a couple of things to help with my camp cooking and decided I needed one last fix of ice cream since it was a hot day and, you know, I'm only human. I guess everyone is only human. Overheard from the car behind as everybody moved through the drive through line:

Speaker: Kawartha Dairy, how can I help you?

Guy in Car: (Huge Sigh) Well, you probably can't. I've got three undecided children in the car here and we're gonna require about three hours.

I was laughing so hard, I thought I was going to hit the car in front of me. I hope the guy didn't hear me as I had the top down on the car. Ice Cream Up, everybody!!!!

# CHAPTER 96

Not so random Sunday, after Saturday if you can find your cup after all the scintillation of a Saturday night, then get on it!

A few Sunday sonnets to titillate and tantalize. They are actually good to use any day. Who am I kidding? Sonnet, my eye. It was Murder Hornet Sunday here today! I kid you not; I killed six, six of the damn things today. I got four before I hardly got going. I could've used the Green Hornet today to fight the black ones. What a superhero! First seen in 1936, the Green Hornet went on to radio, television, comic book, and movie fame. I think he could've shown up here in about 1968 and dealt with these guys right away before they had a chance to live long and prosper. I think there's a nest . . . I see you rolling your eyes out there. I know there's a nest, but it's finding the moth****** Did I just say moth? I meant hornet.

I went from cero (zero) to uno (one); dos (two); tres (three); cuatro (four); cinco (five); seis (six). I'm telling you, all the dudes coming tomorrow had better have their eyes open and their mouths closed. Maybe the shed can take over Hornet Hovering. I think a BOLO is needed. "One Adam 12, see the woman on the corner waving an ineffectual fly swatter madly at anything that flies by her head. Be on the lookout for hornets, large black flying butt ugly things." Bring the Green Lantern with you so you can see them and he can wave his magic ring around and cast them out like so many locusts.

In between swatting soirées, buddy B dropped by for a distant beverage and the other night on my way home, I saw an old friend in town I hadn't seen for years and we chatted distantly like no time had ever passed. Love that!

So, is there any input out there on the output of these damn hornets? I think spray might be in order if I could just figure out how they're getting in. I don't want to learn how to count higher in Spanish, I really don't. Just send the whole Justice League. I'll feed them, get them cocktails, and they can work their good versus evil stuff and make them gone. Failing that, maybe Scotty could beam them up. He could land them in Naked Time, Star Trek, Season 1, Episode 4 where the crew comes in contact with a deadly virus and McCoy develops an antidote just in the nick of time. That would help, wouldn't it? Thrusters on Full, Mr. Scott!

I can't wait to see what tomorrow's upheaval of the house has in store.

Siete (seven); ocho (eight); nueve (nine); diez (ten) . . . Maybe there's an antidote . . .

# CHAPTER 97

Just like everything else in my world, everything seems to happen at once. Rip, wreck, remove, yank, pull, pitch, pile. With a side of scrape, paint, seal for good measure. Pooped. Tired, not the other kind, silly. The Painter dudes, kitchen guy, and Amy & me. Talk about distance. Couldn't get more distant from the front outside to the kitchen inside until the kitchen ended up in various pieces and copious piles in the back yard. Nice and close to the fire pit. There's enough firewood for the next pandemic. So much of it was punky, old and water damaged. Over time and the obvious plumbing issues that must've occurred, I was very glad to have made this decision. The shredded remnants of a mouse nest in a minced up mangled tangle of mail from 1982 found tucked under the counter tells me that things were long overdue for overhaul.

No actual nests of any kind, flying or scurrying were unearthed; however, the prancing and pawing of each of our little hooves coupled with whoops of joy, meant that we had discovered plank flooring under all the old stuff. When the carpet comes out, it will be refinished and sealed up! Big huge Woohoo! Most of what came to light was positive in that there has been no damage to the structure or support of the house, however, there are cosmetic upgrades that can be done so that is just awesome! I'm so excited that it is all happening!

The painting is coming along outside as well. The front windows, the worst job, is underway and the twelve-plus porch windows will be sort of like new. Well, it's fitting. I'm not new and very sort-of, so I think we go together. Like birds of a feather, Heather . . . 😊. If I had a dollar for every time . . .

I'm so thrilled with the progress so far. The wood floor underneath the whole kitchen is a wonderful bonus find. I can't wait to see it uncovered.

I might just survive this after all. Don't tell the shed, it thought it was getting some cupboards to hide its dirty little secrets and unscrupulous mind.

One cupboard might be spared. The one hanging from the ceiling by chains. Fitting, isn't it?

# CHAPTER 98

Grab your coffee on the fly, don't miss the news as it roars by!

So much sawing, roping, cutting, wrangling going on, I thought I was at a rodeo. It's not my first one, you know.

I have paint colours, quantities, a list of stuff to get and an appointment with screen friends to discuss the back porch. The bunkie will be pleased, it will improve its view. I will see how it goes, it might have to wait until next year. That would be ok, even a hurricane can have too many prevailing winds. It might give me time to recover from this year. I know, I know, there's no pleasing the Shed with anything anyway.

The paint guys, from R.A. Painting, took a quick look in the window to see about storage and backed stealthily away, not wanting to upset any apple carts, if I even had one around. What is an apple cart, anyway? Does anybody have one anymore?

Apple pie, apple crumble, apple of your eye . . . but cart? I think the correct saying today would be apple truck if you're moving the darn things around. I've got no truck with apple carts.

I think the Baylands here are having their own sandstorm. At least at my humble abode. The dust, wood chips and tree limbs are everywhere. That tree in the tower? It's almost gone. The kitchen from the end wall, cabinets are going up, up, up!! Excitement abounds!

I am all but useless, since I'm not a cabinet hanger or tree cutter. I can paint but these guys are doing it better than I could. That would, indeed, explain why they're doing it and not me. I think my time is better spent right now writing this, to keep y'all abreast of the latest greatest breaking news as it develops. The cabinets are amazing. What a difference a day makes . . . twenty-four little hours. It feels like forty-four, but who's counting? I think we've all been counting for about four months. We did find where the murder hornets are getting in. Every knot hole, crack and seam out of alignment on the whole damn house. Sealing everything up will solve it. I can't wait. Otherwise *Murder by the Bay* could be the title of the next book. Or even this one, I'm not picky. As long as the gosh darned things disappear like a wicked witch in a bucket of water.

Speaking of same—books, not witches, follow along now, it's not that hard. It was decided to make it longer, so exiting will take longer. That's ok. It's not like any of us are going anywhere fast. There may not be an end in sight at the moment for our current state of world affairs but the kitchen wall is marching along famously. I think the Shed is jealous. First, wood cabinets coming outside that go nowhere near its doors then a new paint job out there just staring it in the face. Jumpin' Jehoshaphat on a piece of toast, if there's enough paint left, we'll paint you too. The volume of grumbling is ferocious. Wait 'til it's time to paint Snow and The Lazy Seven. Whoa, good thing for all of us the Shed can't see that side of the house. Then you want to see what gets carted away and who gets trucked.

# CHAPTER 99

Mawnin! Happy July 1st Canada!

I hope everyone had a happenin' Eh Day with family and/or friends or all three, hee hee.

Coffee or tea, let's look over there,

See what was done to the hurricane's lair.

It was another Big Bay day here at the local Oh My Gawd, what's next?

Since yesterday's flurry of fixation along with a plethora of paint, it seems our modest heroine has attained yet another level in the household game of F.O.R.D. (Fix Or Repair Daily).

As noted in a prior tome, this is the activity around here for the foreseeable, if not, inevitable future. Today's little pastiche of practicality encompassed some additional help and hope for the gardens. Sadly neglected while other areas experienced their time of need, it was their turn.

Shed: "Was not."

Bunkie: "Was too."

Little Shed (LS) to Big Shed (BS): "They might've been . . . don't yell at me."

Snow and the Seven Loafers, amongst themselves: "I don't know . . . you see anything wrong? Me neither . . . nonsense, all of it. Shaddup, I'm tryna sleep."

The Car: "I think we all need to just calm the heck down and wash our hubcaps."

So, as you can see, since the community was busy arguing amongst themselves, nothing else was getting done. The Painter dudes accompanied on trowel and trimmers by Lor, Princess of Earthly Repair, arrived like a tailwind after a tornado and got to work.

So much progress has been made that neighbours were stopping by to comment and compliment on the house and how great it's looking, how the colour is making such a difference and how it just pops now, looking friendlier and happy!

That tree in the tower like so much Rapunzel hair? Gone except for one teeny weeny piece that has grown into the rungs and refuses to leave. The windows are popping brightly like corn in the fire and the trim is just finishing the whole thing off like a good glass of port in the drawing room after Sunday dinner.

It was not a kitchen day today so no updates except our heroine is freakin' amazed!

Lor made hay out of haystacks outside and mincemeat out of the mess around the back deck. Looking like somebody might actually care about the place now.

BS: "Does not."

Bunkie: "Does too."

LS: "I think it kinda maybe is going to be ok."

BS: "Is not."

Everybody Else: "Shaddup!!!!!!"

F.O.R.D. The game the whole family can play, available wherever older houses are sold. F.O.R.D. Bring one home today, just make sure to visit your little local shop on the way for some tasty treats to help the spoon full of sugar and that medicine go down.

Spoons and vodka: not included.

# CHAPTER 100

Oh my goodness, one hundred stories!

It's a centennial celebration! This could require more than coffee ☕ 🍸. One hundred little missives of dubious delight here by the Bay. Thanks so very much for tuning in!

Today was celebratory in several ways. Besides being busy, the Shed was quiet. I could almost just sign off now at leave it at that. The Shed behaved—thanks for coming. It must've known it would get grounded, or even worse, painted yellow if it didn't smarten up. The guys have stayed away from its crusty countenance since the other day. Many compliments have been received from folks for the exterior work around the house. Neighbours are calling, stopping by, all with lovely things to say. The hood is lookin' good! Much more outside stuff has been done and more of the inside is getting ready to go. Yeehaw, indeed! It's fitting, in a celebratory way, to share some other interesting fun stuff that happened.

I had mentioned last week or so, I think, about meeting a neighbour for the first time. The days do run into each other like a race car in a parking lot. It's tough to keep track sometimes. I met up with my neighbour today and learned a bit more history. His family ancestors settled nearby from Ireland and had a number of farms in the area. One of those farms was here. The area behind our road held the farmhouse and barn and the young lads of the Bay used to play there, long after it was no more than a shell. What a haven of exploration for a young boy! Hours and hours spent exploring the remnants of the family home in those carefree childhood days at the lake. I also learned house was actually built earlier than the others so it is most likely between ninety and one hundred years old, rather than the eighty years I had earlier thought. It might explain why the Shed is so grumpy. His great uncle built this cottage first, then later built the forty or so other properties that encompass the hamlet, his own family cottage being built on the last empty lot. Regarding the sawmill, he remembers stories of plenty of sawdust lining the floor of the bay, so deep a six-foot-six-inch tall man walked across the bottom of the Bay without going under. The other homes did not have water access and he has the deed which gave the park and beach to the Association from the folks living in my house around 1961. A long, long time ago.

Thanks for indulging my periodic brief trips down memory lane. Without memories, we wouldn't arrive at today. One hundred memories, experiences, and adventures. I hope you enjoyed them.

Stay tuned for one hundred more.

CPSIA information can be obtained
at www.ICGtesting.com
Printed in the USA
BVHW072015200221
600662BV00002B/77

9 781525 582899